BEHAVIOR ANALYSIS
OF
CHILD DEVELOPMENT

BEHAVIOR ANALYSIS
OF
CHILD DEVELOPMENT

BY
Sidney W. Bijou
UNIVERSITY OF ARIZONA

AND

Donald M. Baer
UNIVERSITY OF KANSAS

Prentice-Hall, Inc., Englewood Cliffs, New Jersey 07632

42263

Library of Congress Cataloging in Publication Data

BIJOU, SIDNEY WILLIAM,
    Behavior analysis and child development.

    (Century psychology series)
    Revision of the 1961 ed. which was issued as Child development, v. 1: A systematic and empirical theory.
    Includes bibliographies and index.
    1. Child psychology.   I. Baer, Donald Merle, joint author.   II. Title.
BF721.B4228   155.4   77–18078
ISBN 0–13–066712–9

Revision of a book formerly entitled
Child Development: A Systematic and Empirical Theory

Printed in the United States of America

10   9   8   7   6   5   4   3   2   1

PRENTICE-HALL INTERNATIONAL, INC., *London*
PRENTICE-HALL OF AUSTRALIA PTY. LIMITED, *Sydney*
PRENTICE-HALL OF CANADA, LTD., *Toronto*
PRENTICE-HALL OF INDIA PRIVATE LIMITED, *New Delhi*
PRENTICE-HALL OF JAPAN, INC., *Tokyo*
PRENTICE-HALL OF SOUTHEAST ASIA PTE. LTD., *Singapore*
WHITEHALL BOOKS LIMITED, *Wellington, New Zealand*

To the many thousand experimental psychologists who have made this volume possible.

CONTENTS

42263

PREFACE

This is a revision of a book published in 1961 on a systematic and empirical theory of human psychological development from the point of view of natural science. These terms are defined in the Introduction of the text. To the reader who looks upon the approach of natural science as the basic method of knowledge, this treatment will simply be an extension of that approach to the analysis of what is popularly called "child psychology." To the reader who holds a different view of theory, this work may offer an example of an alternative approach. And for the reader with no particular outlook on the methodological problem of what constitutes a scientific statement, this volume will at least provide a set of concepts and principles useful in the description and organization of child behavior and development. We would add that this system of concepts also offers a significant degree of *explanation*.

This volume is written for the student who studies behavior and development and has little or no background in psychology. Consequently, we have included only the most basic terms and principles. Those details or behavior mechanisms that generate so much heat among theorists have been largely omitted. The descriptions of behavior changes which are common to all of their arguments have been retained, stated in terms designed to be simple, clear, and complete. The examples supporting each concept are intended to clarify and generalize its meaning, not to document its validity.

In fact, little effort is made to document these principles. Occasional references to research findings are for illustrative purposes. This decision is based on three considerations. First, an attempt to validate these concepts would be contrary to the objective of presenting an easily read-able account of the theory itself. The presentation would have to be longer, more detailed, and more technical. Second, the data upon which a theory like this is built are well summarized in several texts designed for that purpose. Some of these are noted in our reference lists.

This revision is basically similar to the original version. However, these theoretical changes should be noted: (1) The concept that behavior is a function of past and present stimuli has been replaced with the concept that a change in any component of an interactional sequence affects all components of that interaction, that is, the emphasis is on interdependent reciprocal interactions, (2) emotion as a pattern of operant and respondent reaction has been replaced with Kantor's concept of a momentary cessation of operant behavior, and (3) affective behavior is analyzed as interactions chained to internal stimulation.

As in the first edition, exposition proceeds from simple to complex processes but the interrelationships are more explicit. Furthermore complex processes not mentioned previously, such as decision making, problem solving, thinking, and biofeedback have been included. In addition, explanations of basic terms such as positive and negative reinforcement and principles such as shaping and stimulus and response generalization have been expanded and diagrams have been included. Finally, there are, throughout the text, more frequent references to practical applications.

Publication of the original volume in 1961 has been followed by three related books. The first one which appeared in 1965 applied the theory to development in infancy (the foundational stage), the second, a collection of readings which also appeared in 1965, presented examples of basic and applied research, and the third, which was published in 1976, applied the theory to development in early childhood (the basic stage). The preparation of these publications undoubtedly helped us to re-evaluate the content and the form of our first offering.

Essentially, the theory presented here brings together the contributions of many psychologists. As before, our most basic debts are to B. F. Skinner, J. R. Kantor, F. S. Keller, and W. N. Shoenfeld. We hope that this application of their work will give additional impetus to the objective analysis of human behavior.

We wish to thank our students and colleagues for their helpful comments and criticism of the first version of the book. With respect to the latter, we are particularly indebted to Jay Birnbrauer, Howard C. Gilhousen, Wendell E. Jeffrey, Lewis P. Lipsitt, Kenneth MacCorquodale, and O. Ivar Lovaas. We also wish to thank our students and colleagues for their suggestions and remarks for the revision. The latter include Rodger K. Bufford, Wayne R. Carroll, Kenneth MacCorquodale, Edward K. Morris, and Joseph A. Parsons.

S. W. B.
D. M. B.

Introduction

We present here an analysis of child development from the natural science point of view. In more general terms, it is an analysis of human psychological development. Our presentation is in the form of a theory, which we shall explain first by clarifying the meaning of the term theory itself and then the two key terms: "psychological development" and "natural science."

THEORY

The first definition of theory listed in *The Random House Dictionary of the Englis'! Language* is "a coherent group of general propositions used as principles of explanation for a class of phenomena." According to this meaning of the term, a theory of psychological development is a set of general propositions (definitions of terms and principles of relationships among the terms) showing the environment-behavior relationships that summarize the particular interactions we observe in a child. So a theoretical statement is not simply a statement of some particular interaction, such as the way a toddler named Betty eats. It is, rather, a statement about many such particular interactions, tied together so that they exemplify a *general principle of development.* For example, we might explain why, in general, toddlers eat with a spoon. A mother consistently feeds her child with a spoon, and so a spoon is always present at feeding times and is available for picking up food. Toddlers have a strong tendency to pick things up and put them in their mouths. When those things are spoons and have food on them, similar occasions are more likely to produce similar putting-in-the-mouth behavior. Here we are making a statement of principles, which (1) shows the essential similarity of the eating situation of most toddlers, (2) introduces a principle of behavior with food as a stimulus following a response, and (3) explains in terms of history why toddlers in this society generally eat with a spoon.

PSYCHOLOGICAL DEVELOPMENT

Psychological development is defined in various ways. In some approaches designated as normative, development is said to be a characteristic if it can be related to age in an orderly or lawful way. In other approaches, development refers simply to the sequence of changes in the life span from conception to death. And in still others, development is said to be characterized by some all-inclusive descriptive principle such as: it is change that proceeds from a state of relative globality to a state of increasing differentiation, articulation, and hierarchic integration. We believe that most definitions are either incomplete or involve terms that defy empirical definitions.

By psychological development we mean *progressive changes in interactions between the behavior of individuals and the events in their environment.* The emphasis here is on changes in interactions. This formulation leads us to expect that any given response may occur or not occur, depending on the current environment. If the response occurs, it will usually change the stimulus properties of that environment for that individual. This change in environmental stimulation may then set the occasion for another response, which probably will effect further changes in the environment, and so on. For example, a man is driving his car on a cloudy day. Suddenly, the sun breaks through the clouds—a change in environmental stimulation. The bright light causes the man to squint, a response that reduces the glare. Squinting requires too much effort for comfort, and narrows the driver's field of vision. These two response-produced changes in stimulation—the strain of partly closing the eyes and the restriction of visibility—lead him to respond further by reaching into the glove compartment for his sunglasses and putting them on.

This example illustrates that individuals interact continuously and endlessly with their environment. In other words, behavior affects environment and environment affects behavior. However, the subject matter of this discussion is psychological development, the progressive changes in environment-behavior interactions that occur with the passage of time from conception to death. Our interest is in changes that take place over periods of days, months, and years. Take the behavior of eating as an example. Eating is a fairly well-defined sequence of responses and stimuli in interaction. For infants, this interaction involves stimulation by the sight and feel of the breast, and by internal changes correlated with the time since the last feeding. Assume that four hours have elapsed since the infant was last fed. As a mother prepares to nurse her baby, the sight of her breast or the feel of her nipple against the baby's cheek gives rise to sucking behavior. Sucking obtains food; thus the effect of this new state of affairs (satiation) is to decrease sucking, which gives rise to other responses, such as looking about, smiling, gurgling, going to sleep, etc. But for the toddler, eating is in most ways a different interaction. Again, the time since the last meal is an important stimulus condition, but now the sight and feel of mother's breast as a stimulus for eating have been replaced by the sight, feel, and smell of things like bacon, cereal, cookies, milk, juice, dishes, spoons, cups, and so on. The response is no longer sucking; it is instead a series of reaching, grasping, and bringing-to-the-mouth responses, all of which provide stimulation to the gums and tongue which gives rise to chewing and swallowing rather than to sucking. The end result is still the same: a change from a situation without food to one with an ample amount of food. However, this change is generally followed by behaviors quite different from those seen in the infant, notably the much more complex behaviors of looking about and vocalizing, perhaps crying to be let out of the baby table, and a low probability of dropping off to sleep.

In the same way, infants display irritable signs of fatigue, and are put to bed by parents; older children, whether fatigued or not, attend to the time of night and their parents wishes, and put themselves to bed; and self-responsible adults attend to their own internal indicators of fatigue and to the work or vacation schedule that they know awaits them the next day, and choose their bed times accordingly.

Similarly, an infant reacts to the loss of an important object by crying; older children look about haphazardly and seek help from parents; adults (at their best) look systematically and intelligently in the places that experience tells them are the likely repositories.

Obviously, then, the infant's eating is one kind of interaction, but the toddler's is another; bedtime is one interaction for infants, a different one for older children, and yet another one for adults; loss is one kind of interaction for a baby, quite another for the older child, and still different for the adult. It is the *changes* in interactions that are of primary concern here. How do they come about? Our answers to this question, and to all other questions relating to changes between behavior and environment with age, maturity, and longer interactional history will make up the body of this volume. In general, the answers will involve changes in the environment, changes in behavior, and the relationships between them.

The simplest view of progressive behavior change is that it comes with age—that growth produces new abilities. This is indeed true, but it is only the beginning of an adequate analysis of how thoroughly behavior change is an interaction between individual and environment (Baer, 1970). For, as age produces growth, and growth yields new abilities, environment reacts. The ability to walk, for example, frees the hands and at the same time makes that part of the world that is two feet off the ground available to the child for the first time. And there are many more provocative stimuli in that part of the world to foster the child's use of those newly emerged abilities. It is as if the environment *encourages* standing. As those abilities flower under this provocation, the child's activities will take on new significance for parents, who now must defend their possessions against infantile curiosity and exploration (often expensive), and who usually will be moved to provide new objects in compensation for the prized ones they take away—cheaper objects, of course, but more to the point, infant-appropriate. Furthermore, they will be moved now, as they have not been previously, to begin the social control of their child. The sound of "No" will be heard in the land, sometimes with contingencies to back it up. As more capabilities emerge from the child (or more accurately, as more capabilities are shaped and extracted from the child's relatively unchoate emerging biological gains), parents' and others' reactions to the child will continue to change: new respect for the child's capability will be developed, and tricycles, baseball equipment, dolls and accessories, pets, etc., will be provided (often just a little too early, which is again provocative in its own way); new assumptions about the child's understanding will grow, and longer and more accurate explanations and requests will be offered to the child; and new impositions of responsibility will be considered reasonable, and reward and punishment for meeting and failing some of those responsibilities will be applied. In one of the most far-reaching of these interactions, when children have sufficient response capability (are well able to walk and run, are reliably toilet trained, have a fair vocabulary, are reasonably manageable by strangers, and so on) in this culture, we change their social environment drastically by enrolling them in school. There, many old interactions are modified, and many new ones are developed. The basic concern in all that is to follow is the understanding of all such interactions of human behavior and environment.

NATURAL SCIENCE

The second key term in our statement of purpose, "natural science," is closely related to the meaning of theory used here. The natural science approach is the study of any natural, lawful, orderly phenomenon by certain methods. These are the methods that characterize scientists and distinguish them from others who also seek knowledge about the same phenomena but use different methods. A philosopher, for example, may reflect on statements that seem fundamental and unquestionable and then deduce from these premises certain conclusions about particular problems. An artist may express implicit reactions in words, painting, sculpture, or music as the artistic truth (at least for the artist). But scientists (as defined here) restrict themselves to a study of *what they can observe* either with the naked eye or with instruments. Their general procedure is to manipulate in an observable way whatever conditions they suspect are important to their problems, and then to observe what changes take place as a result. They relate these changes to their manipulation of conditions, as orderly dependencies: the speed of a falling body depends on the time since it was released; the volume of a gas depends on its temperature and the pressure exerted by its container; pulse rate depends on breathing rate; the skill with which toddlers can eat with a spoon depends on the number of times they have previously managed to scoop up food with it.

In some branches of natural science, such as astronomy or subatomic physics, the subject matter is not directly manipulable. The investigator must necessarily then draw inferences or state hypotheses about functional relationships and make predictions based on them. The accuracy of the predictions tests the soundness of the inferences. Because of its success in the physical sciences, this procedure, frequently called the hypothetico-deductive method, has gained tremendous prestige and has led many psychologists to claim that it is *the* scientific method. In actual practice, scientists sometimes follow the hypothetico-deductive procedure, sometimes the inductive procedure, and sometimes a combination of the two, depending on the sophistication of the science and the problem being investigated. When the science is young and the subject matter is observable and directly manipulable, as in psychology, the inductive method is particularly suitable.

Scientists sometimes gather information on a group of instances and sometimes on individual instances, depending on the kind of information they seek (Sidman, 1960). Methods yielding data on groups of objects, individuals, or events are particularly serviceable when the question requires information (1) from a survey, such as, "How many handicapped preschool children are there in the counties in California north of San Francisco?"; (2) about a correlation, such as, "What is the relationship between the socioeconomic status of young parents and their educational attainment?"; (3) about functional relationships among averages, such as "Is spaced practice more effective in rote learning than concentrated practice?"; or (4) confirming or disproving a hypothesis about hypothetical concepts, such as, "Does logic change with training?" On the other hand, methods resulting in information about individual instances are particularly fruitful when we want to know about the functional relationships between circumstances and the behavior of an individual, such as, "Is the rate of self-destructive behavior of a psychotic child influenced by the degree of social demands imposed?"

The point is that regardless of the purpose of their research, natural scientists deal with observable events. Therefore, it is traditional for them to say that toddlers develop skillful techniques of eating with a spoon largely because of past successes in getting food that way, a statement that refers to observable events in a segment of any child's interactional history. In general, a patently observable phenomenon is that behavior which produces food tends to grow stronger. To say that children learn to eat with a spoon because of an inner urge to grow up, or because they want to be like adults, is to appeal to something unobservable (an "urge," a "want"). If psychology is to accrue the benefits of the scientific method, such statements are handicapping.

Our approach to the study of development is one of three or four current approaches in contemporary psychology.[1] Admittedly, we have made a choice in selecting an approach that supports a natural science conception rather than one of the others that would permit statements about hypothetical unobservable phenomena. But we point to the advantages: (1) relative simplicity, (2) the frequency of fruitful results, and (3) freedom from logical tangles that ultimately are illusory.

Our usage of theory dovetails with the natural science conception of science because our theoretical statements are *generalized propositions about observable interactions between the environment and behavior.* How one generalizes statements of this kind deserves clarification, because it is important in the account of child development that will follow. By way of illustration, consider an inductive principle that will figure repeatedly in any analysis of child development: the reinforcement rule

[1]Some psychologists, such as Roger Brown, say that psychology is the study of mind; others, such as Freud, that it is the study of the mind as revealed by behavior.

for strengthening a response-stimulus relationship. We can illustrate this rule with a laboratory rat in a small, specially constructed enclosure. The animal has been without food for 24 hours. The enclosure is a simple room, containing only a lever protruding from one wall at a height easy for the rat to investigate, and a dispenser from which small pellets of food can be ejected at any time. As an arbitrary case in point, we assume an interest in the animal's behavior toward the lever. The lever's construction is such that it will move downward a fraction of an inch if pressed, but is otherwise immobile. In the process of what seems to be exploration, the animal is likely to press that lever downward, perhaps three times an hour on the average. If we now arrange the mechanism controlling the enclosure so that every lever press produces a food pellet from the dispenser, lever-pressing will quickly become more frequent, regular, and efficient. The animal's behavior of lever-pressing is now in an apparently forceful interaction with the environment: it has become a part of feeding, and while the effects of the animal's 24-hour food deprivation last, this newly established style of feeding will continue (especially in the absence of an easier alternative). The lever-pressing behavior will be said to have been strengthened in this situation; that is, it occurs now much more often than before because of this history.

We may sum up these observations in a general statement: Our animal can be taught lever-pressing by food reinforcement. The statement implies that we could have done the same thing at any time with this animal, which makes it a small induction. We do not actually know that we could have done the same thing at any time; we only know that it was successful *this* time. But we suppose from past experience that rats are much the same throughout much of their lives, barring the special phenomena of very early infancy and senility (during which times they are still susceptible to reinforcement, but perhaps only through specialized techniques). Indeed, to say that "rats are much the same" suggests a somewhat more extensive induction than the one above, specifically: Rats can be taught lever-pressing by food reinforcement.

Several thousand experiments, basically like the one just described, have allowed similar inductions about a tremendous range of subject species, including humans; and about lever-pressing and a multitude of other responses, including language; and in a myriad of settings, including homes and schools; and with a diversity of reinforcers ranging from biological necessities of life such as food and water to culturally defined events such as approval and prestige, and aesthetic events such as music and art. A simple collation of these facts would be: Some organisms can be taught some responses by some kinds of reinforcement. A modest induction of the same facts might be: Organisms can be taught many diverse responses by reinforcement. A daring induction is that: Any organism can be taught any response by reinforcement, and this one we know is incorrect in saying "any response." The exceptions are discussed as a general case in Chapter 4, and ways to circumvent these exceptions are discussed in Chapter 11 as cases of self-management, biofeedback, and problem solving. Then we should retreat to a less daring induction: Many organisms can be taught many responses by reinforcement and its practical corrolary, try solving behavior problems by reinforcing their desirable components.

Here we have the present status of the reinforcement rule. It is a summary of many, many well-proved facts, and it is also an induction that goes beyond them to suggest that the uniformity with which they are found to be true suggests strongly that they are generally (but not universally) true. In that the induction goes further than proven fact, it is a statement of theory; in that it goes beyond fact only to suggest that an observed generality is probably more general than the cases observed so far, it is empirically based and characteristic of a natural science approach. The ultimate evaluation of this approach, relying as uniformly as possible on inductions of just this character, will depend on the adequacy with which it accounts for the psychological development of humans.

REFERENCES

BAER, D.M., An age-irrelevant concept of development. *Merrill-Palmer Quarterly of Behavior and Development,* 1970, *16,* 238–245.

SIDMAN, M., *Tactics of Scientific Research.* New York: Basic Books, 1960

2

The Context
of Development Theory

A theory of human psychological development involves a description of terms (concepts) and statements of the relationships among them (principles). In a natural science approach, the terms are limited to the observable, recordable instances of the behavior of children in relation to the specific observable events that make up their environments. To integrate this approach with other areas in psychology and related fields, we focus on one stream of contemporary psychology—behavioral psychology—and indicate its relationship with animal biology on the one hand, and cultural anthropology on the other.

Most of the discussion that follows is not to be construed as an elaboration of the theory described in Chapter 1. It is concerned with some of the assumptions on which the theory and its investigatory methods rest. A complete set of the underpinning "givens" would constitute the *philosophy of science* of the approach which is called *behaviorism*. Variations in assumptions found among behavioral approaches earn variations in designation such as interbehaviorism, methodological behaviorism, and radical behaviorism.

THE NATURE OF CONTEMPORARY BEHAVIORAL PSYCHOLOGY

Psychology is a part of the scientific activity of our culture. It is that subdivision of scientific work that analyzes the interaction of the behavior of organisms, human and infrahuman, with environmental stimuli, at least behavioral psychology does. Psychology is divided into abnormal, clinical, social, educational, industrial, comparative, physiological, and developmental psychology. Developmental psychology, the branch of particular interest here, is sometimes called genetic psychology because it focuses on the origins and evolution of behavior. (This alternate desig-

nation should not be confused with genetics, the part of biology that deals
with heredity and variation in the structure and functioning of animals
and plants.) Developmental psychology focuses on the progressions and
regressions in interactions between the behaviors of individuals and environmental events. In other words, it concentrates on *the effects of
past interactions on present interactions, or the developmental status of
an individual.*

We know that other sciences also analyze the interaction of organisms,
human and infrahuman, with environmental events. But we distinguish
them from the domain of psychology by the way we define the three
critical terms: environmental stimuli, behavior, and environment-
behavior interaction.

Environmental stimuli of special interest to behavioral psychology are
the observable physical, chemical, biological, and social events that
interact with the behavior of an individual. "Some of these are to be
found in the hereditary history of the individual, including his member-
ship in a given species as well as his personal endowment. Others arise
from his physical environment, past or present" (Skinner, 1972a, p. 260).
Such events may be measured by scales, rulers, stop watches, decibel
indicators, illuminometers, and temperature gauges. The results of such
measurement describe the *physical* dimensions of stimuli. These same
events may also be measured by the changes in the behaviors of individuals,
that is, changes in the frequency of occurrence, amplitude, or latency of
their responses. The results of this assessment are the functional dimensions of stimuli. (The difference between the physical and functional
dimensions of stimuli will be discussed later in greater detail.)

Behavior of particular interest here is "the observable activity of the
organism, as it moves about, stands still, seizes objects, pushes and pulls,
makes sounds, gestures, and so on." (Skinner, 1972a, pp. 260-261). In
other words, psychology concentrates on the behavior of an individual as
a total functioning organism. To say that the subject matter of this branch
of science is the behavior of a total functioning individual does not mean
that investigators always attempt to observe, measure, and relate all of
an organism's responses taking place at one time. On the contrary, history
has shown that many significant contributions have come from studies
that have focused on only a few measures. In practice, the number of
responses observed in the stimulus-response interaction is largely dependent
on the purpose of a particular study. A study of the knee-jerk reflex will
be limited to one response and one type of antecedent stimulus (tap on
the patellar tendon); a study of the startle response again will focus on

one response complex and its components (all or some of which can occur, depending on the effectiveness of the stimulus) and on a wide variety
of auditory, visual, or tactual "startling" stimuli; and a study of problem-
solving by high school students will include a wide range of responses to
an equally wide range of stimuli.

Responses and their products, such as spoken and written language,
are, like stimuli, measured by physical instruments such as stop watches
and decibel gauges. The results are the *physical* dimensions of responses.
And, also like stimuli, responses are measured by what they do to the
functional environment, as the flick of a wall switch produces light in a
dark room or the request for a newspaper from a newsboy results in his
handing you a newspaper. These are the *functional* dimensions of
responses, the dimensions we are most interested in and the ones we shall
talk about repeatedly in this volume.

Then it should come as no surprise that stimuli and responses are
analyzed in behavioral psychology in *exactly the same way*. Both are
treated as sets of conditions in an interactional setting. Remember that
most interactions are social, that is, the responses of one person serve as
stimuli for another person or persons and, as such, these stimuli must be
analyzed in the same way as those from the physical aspect of the environment. We should also point out that because of the *mutual* relationship
between stimuli and responses in a behavioral system, a functional definition of stimuli assumes a functional definition of responses. We shall discuss the nature of responses further in the next chapter.

The *interaction* between stimuli and behavior is always an *interdependent* relationship. The behavior of an individual is continuously
being changed by the action of stimuli. At no time does an individual
stand around passively waiting to be stimulated by the environment. Such
a notion is contrary to the notion of the functional properties of the
environment and the behavior of an individual. The change in behavior
is referred to variously as reflex, learning, adjustment, maturation,
development, habilitation, and adaptation. Stimuli, in turn, are constantly
being acted on and changed by the behavior of an individual or individuals
in concert. Humankind relentlessly changes the environment, trying to
enhance growth, development, and survival, for self and for posterity.
Thus, the stimulating conditions that constitute the environment produce
changes in behavior; these behavior changes alter the environment; the
altered environment (with other, more stable influences, such as the sea-
sons of the year) produces further behaviors that again modify the
environment, etc., resulting in the construction of unique cultures (modi-

fied environments) on one hand, and unique individual psychological developments on the other.

Basic and Applied Behavioral Psychology

We have been describing basic behavioral psychology. The question is often asked: What is the difference between basic and applied behavioral psychology? A great deal has been written about the similarities and differences between the two and, in many treatments, social and economic issues have been raised that cloud the relationship. Actually, the difference between the two areas is not always easy to discern. However, these distinctions may be made: (1) The subject matter is the same, and methods of investigation and the procedures for analyzing and interpreting findings to guard against cultural intrusions are the same (Baer, Wolf, and Risley, 1968, *1*, 91-97); (2) The objectives of investigation are different. In basic behavior psychology, the objective is to rearrange a set of conditions and see what happens to behavior and to the other conditions in the situation. In applied behavioral psychology (or behavioral technology, behavior modification, or applied behavior analysis), the objective is to rearrange a set of conditions and see whether the results answer a socially important problem in education, treatment, child rearing practices, counseling, guidance, community living, industry, and the like; and (3) Many of the findings of basic research are applied to the problems of everyday living and many of the problems generated from practical application become problems for basic research (Skinner, 1972b, pp. 1-6).

THE INTERDEPENDENCIES AMONG BEHAVIORAL PSYCHOLOGY, ANIMAL BIOLOGY, AND CULTURAL ANTHROPOLOGY

It will clarify the domain of behavioral psychology to review its relationships to two neighboring branches of science: animal biology and cultural anthropology. Knowledge from animal biology is pertinent to a better understanding of the structures and mechanisms that are a part of a response to stimuli, and to the range of responses that exists at a given time and their stimuli. Knowledge from anthropology is pertinent to a clearer appreciation of how response capabilities come under social control, and what kinds of responses will be selected from the biologically available range for control, including occasional floutings of well-established biological mechanisms, as when the children of some groups are deliberately taught to endure extreme pain without escaping. Although the lines separating the three fields are fuzzy, each field does have certain discernible features, and each field is dependent on the other two for information and advances in methodology. The differentiating features are those we shall stress.

Psychology and Animal Biology

Animal biology may be defined as the study of the origin, reproduction, structure, and function of animal life. To a large extent, this discipline is concerned with the interaction between organisms and organic and non-organic materials, and with the consequent changes in the structure and functioning of their parts.[1] As we have said, behavioral psychology is primarily concerned with the interaction of an individual, as a *unified and integrated behavior system,* with environmental events. It is apparent, therefore, that every psychological sequence is also a biological sequence; it is correlated with interactions between stimuli and muscles, organs, and connecting systems (circulatory, nervous, etc.) of an organism. Both sequences take place *simultaneously.* Which one attracts the attention of investigators depends foremost on whether their views of causation typically relate the entire organism to its controlling environment, or whether they see the entire organism as a complex arrangement of its separate parts. Either attitude is legitimate, but incomplete without the other. Some scientists have attempted to follow both viewpoints simultaneously, in both biology and psychology.

The behavior of an infant during feeding is a case in point. From the psychological point of view, the important behaviors are grasping the nursing bottle, getting the nipple into the mouth, and sucking. But it is also necessary to take account of the present environmental conditions (appearance, weight, and contents of the bottle, convenience of the bottle for tiny hands, number of hours since last feeding, etc.) and of historical

[1] A noteworthy exception is ecology. Ecology is a branch of biology which deals with the relationships between the organism as a whole and its entire environment, which includes the behavior of other organisms in that environment. This definition, as some ecologists have pointed out, makes psychology, anthropology, sociology, history, economics, and political science mere subdivisions of ecology. (In practice, however, the ecologist concentrates on such variables as the population of each species living in an environment, food supply, and the effect of its changing numbers upon other species in the same environment.) This example re-emphasizes the overlapping nature of psychology, biology, and other branches of sciences dealing with living organisms.

events (number of times in the past that the sight of the bottle was followed by reaching, grasping, and thrusting the smaller end of the bottle into the mouth and getting milk; the regularity of the number of hours between feedings, etc.). The same act might be studied from the biological point of view involving the activity of the digestive system from the moment the milk enters the infant's mouth to the time its waste products are eliminated.

The fact that psychological and organismic events take place at the same time does not mean that one class of events *causes* the other, that is, that organismic variables cause psychological reactions, or vice versa. The causes of a specific class of behavior, psychological or organismic, must be determined separately by an analysis of the specific environmental conditions that apply. Of course, organismic conditions often do play a part in determining psychological reactions, just as psychological events often contribute to producing organismic responses. (Indeed, the latter possibility is the main concern of psychosomatic medicine and the so-called psychogenic disorders.) On page 13 we stated that the environmental events of psychological behavior include the organismic variables of interest to the biologist. These stimuli, like the other important stimuli (physical, chemical, and social), *contribute* to causation. None of the four classes is necessarily singled out as the *sole* determinant for any psychological reaction. It is true, certainly, that for many psychological reactions the major condition is organismic. For example, a sharp pain in the stomach from food poisoning may play the major role in producing the behaviors of clutching at the stomach and frantically telephoning the doctor. But in telephoning the doctor, it is obvious that a certain history of interaction with social stimuli is involved; otherwise the person would be unable to dial a telephone and would know nothing of doctors and their function in dealing with such pain. Other psychological reactions are caused primarily by social stimuli ("You're welcome" in response to "Thanks"), or by physical stimuli ("Ouch!" to a cut finger), or by chemical stimuli ("Phew" to an unpleasant odor).

In each instance of behavior, a proper and complete account of the cause-and-effect relationships involved should include *all* classes of stimuli acting on the individual and their relevant interactional histories. Attending only to the dominant environmental event is bound to result in incomplete and oversimplified accounts of functional relationships. The occasionally encountered dictum, especially in the psychoanalytic literature, that motivation is the cause of all behavior is an example of a much too restricted account.

At the same time, to contend that biological interactions are not the sole nor invariable causes of psychological events clearly does not diminish the *interdependence* of biology and psychology. Psychologists are interested in the findings of biologists on the organs and systems of the human body that participate with other variables in determining psychological interactions. (For example, does the hypothalamus mediate rage and anger?) Developmental psychologists seek from biologists information on the motor and sensory equipment of the child at various stages of development. (For example, are the taste buds of a preschool child comparable in sensitivity to those of an adult?) Prominent among the factors that determine whether a response will occur is the availability of the organismic equipment necessary to perform the act. (Learning to walk is dependent in part on the strength of the leg bones and muscles and the relative weights of the head and torso.)

Psychology and Cultural Anthropology

We turn now to the relationships between psychology and the social sciences, particularly cultural anthropology. Certainly the conditions determining psychological behavior and development are for the most part social. These influences, which begin at birth and vary widely throughout the life span, include all the conditions that involve people, directly or indirectly. People make all sorts of demands ("Brush your teeth in the morning and again at night" and "You have to make a living when you grow up") and set all sorts of occasions for behavior ("It's time for lunch"); people approve behavior ("Atta girl") and are present when social and physical hurts and restraints are removed ("You took that like a man"); people disapprove and punish behavior directly ("For talking back, go to the principal's office") and bring about nonsocial painful consequences ("Open your mouth so I can drill that tooth"); people prescribe the forms of behavior appropriate in significant social situations ("Put your napkin in your lap") and set the level of skill required for tasks ("If your composition has more than one spelling error, you will flunk"); and people create many or most of the physical objects of the culture that play a part in shaping behavior desired by the culture (furniture, roads, cars, tools, signs, and napkins).

Cultural anthropology, the study of humans and their products, is devoted to analyzing social organizations, industrial techniques, art, religions, languages, laws, customs, and manners. Knowledge of the origins, changes, and range of cultural events is indispensable to developmental psychology in relating social variables and behavior. For example, cultural anthropology analyzes the adult-child and child-peer relationships, role specializations (mothering functions, provider of economic goods, head of local community, etc.), and social subgroupings (socio-economic class, urban-rural, etc.) of a society. Another example, and an area of considerable current interest because of its promise to shed more light on the formation of the patterns of social behavior ("personality"), is child-rearing practices in primitive as well as in complex modern societies. Specifically, these include mother and family activities in initiating an infant into its society through the prescribed procedures that are part of feeding, toilet training, cleaning, dressing, sex training, and aggression training.

SUMMARY

We cannot study psychological development in isolation from its biology and its culture because it is part of biology and always occurs in relation to a culture. And we cannot study it properly knowing only its biology and its culture because development depends on interactional mechanisms that are investigated best by the disciplinary techniques of experimental psychology. The study of those mechanisms as limited, constrained, and impelled by biological and cultural phenomena is more nearly a characterization of a discipline of psychological development. Thus, we note that it is a biological truism that metabolism creates waste products and that waste products are excreted for the health of the organism. Furthermore, we note that feces, once excreted, nevertheless remain a long-term health hazard for most complex organisms in that they breed the disease-causing bacteria that often cause death. Yet it is culture that decrees a solution to that problem, even to the extent of insisting that feces have magical, religious, or aesthetic characteristics that require their ritualistic disposition. But the decreeing of a ritual does not guarantee that it will be performed. It is the psychological mechanisms of interactional change, imposed at culture's direction on a biological problem, that constitute a successful solution of this problem in those societies that survive.

REFERENCES

BAER, D.M., WOLF, .M.M. AND RISLEY, T.R., Some current dimensions of applied behavior analysis. *Journal of Applied Behavior Analysis,* 1968, *1,* 91-97.

SKINNER, B.F., *Cumulative Record.* (3rd ed.). Englewood Cliffs, N.J.: Prentice-Hall, 1972(a), p. 260.

SKINNER, B.F., Some relations between behavior modifrcation and basic research. In S.W. Bijou and E. Ribes-Inesta (Eds.), *Behavior Modification: Issues and Extensions.* New York: Academic Press, 1972(b), pp. 1-6.

3

The Child, the Environment, and Their Continuous Interactions

To elaborate on a behavioral theory of human development, we shall analyze (1) the behavior of a child as a psychological entity, (2) the environment of development, (3) the continuous and reciprocal interaction between the behavior of a child and the environment, and (4) the stages of this continuous and reciprocal interaction.

THE CHILD

Children are conceptualized psychologically as clusters of responses and sources of internal stimuli (organismic stimuli). The responses are interrelated to each other and are continuously interacting with stimuli from both internal and external sources. The sources of internal stimuli are the children's physiological functioning, and their motor and verbal behavior.

Clusters of Responses

The number and kinds of responses children are capable of making at any point of their lives are tremendous. Developmental psychologists have attempted to group the behaviors of young children according to various conceptions of personality. Cognitive psychologists claim that children's observable behaviors reveal mental processes such as knowing, willing, feeling, or thinking; psychoanalysts claim that the same behaviors reveal the growth and activities of the id, ego, and superego parts of personality. And normative psychologists, such as Gesell (1954), assert that children's observable behaviors, consisting of motor, social, linguistic, emotional, and intellectual components, reveal the development of their minds as do organs in their various embryonic stages. In our treatment, children's behaviors are treated as important data in their own right. That is to say, we take the position that children's behaviors are not determined by hypothetical mental processes or personalities, but by *species characteristics, biological maturation, and the history of interaction with the particular environment from the moment of conception.* The relationships between responses and species and maturational characteristics are of particular interest to the biologist; the relationship between responses and history of interactions with the environment is of particular interest to the developmental psychologist. It is therefore necessary that we dwell somewhat on an analysis of behavior in interaction with the environment.

Remember that behavioral psychology is concerned with observable behavior which is analyzed in terms of both its physical and functional properties. Measurement of the physical aspects of behavior, or the products of behavior (e.g., vocalizations, language, drawings, or writings), poses no more of a problem for psychology than the measurement of any other physical phenomenon. However, measurement of the functional aspects of behavior, or the products of behavior, is fraught with difficulties, as the history of psychology will attest (Kantor, 1963 and 1969).

The functional aspect of behavior, or response function. We begin our analysis of behavior with the notion that functionally speaking there are two large classes of responses: respondents and operants (Skinner, 1938, p. 80). Respondent behavior is strengthened or weakened by the stimuli that *precede* the behavior; operant behavior is strengthened or weakened by the stimuli that *follow* the behavior. Note that the distinction between the two classes of behavior is entirely in the time relationship between a response and its functional stimulus.

Respondent behavior, which includes the contraction of the pupils to bright light and salivation to food in the mouth, alters the individual in ways that reduce deprivation of stimuli or aversive stimulation and thereby maintain physiological equilibrium. Respondent behavior accommodates the individual to specific environmental situations. Contraction of the pupils to bright light reduces the light entering the eye and thereby facilitates visual interactions (external processes); it also guards retinal cells against damage from intense stimulation. Salivation produces a fluid that mixes with food, facilitating its subsequent digestion. Each respondent has a function specifically correlated with a stimulus function, some given in the nature of the organism and some acquired through past interactions.

Operant behavior, which includes manipulation, walking, talking, problem solving, drawing, and writing, alters the environment and thereby increases the probability of other behavior. Thus, flipping a switch (operant behavior) turns on the room light and enables a food-deprived individual to approach the refrigerator and obtain food (other forms of operant behavior). And talking, among other things, may alter the environment through the activities of other people, such as getting a toy by asking Mother to bring it. As with respondent behavior, each class of operant behavior is correlated with a stimulus function, some given in the nature of the organism and some acquired through past interactions. We cannot elaborate further on response functions, operant and respondent, until we discuss stimulus functions in our treatment of the environment.

The concept of response class. We shall now add an important elaboration of the meaning of response. If a response were observed in great detail each time it occurred, it would quickly become clear that the response is never exactly the same each time it occurs. Suppose, for example, that a child is being taught the relatively simple skill of putting on a hat. Sometimes the hat will be picked up with one hand, sometimes the other, sometimes with both. Some of the grasping responses may involve all the fingers and the thumb; others may involve only one, two, or three fingers opposing the thumb(s). Sometimes the hat will be picked up by the brim, sometimes by the crown or band or lining. We see that there is an infinite variety to the detailed variations possible in even such a simple response. Thus, when the child learns what we call one response—putting on a hat—in fact an almost innumerable collection of responses has been learned, if we care to study them in the detail they present. So, in general, when we refer to a response, remember that almost without exception, we are referring to a *class of responses.* By response class we mean all those varied forms of response that accomplish the same function—in this example, all the ways that children can get their hats on their heads. Often, the members of a response class will be highly similar variations on a simple theme, as in the above example. In other cases, the members of a response class may have little physical resemblance to one another; all that they have in common is that they have the same effect in the environment, or respond to the same event in the environment. A response class for convincing people may contain rational arguments, pleading techniques, and blustering techniques, or a response class requesting a person to come to you may include beckoning, a written note, or a verbal utterance (Winokur, 1976).

Sources of Stimuli

As noted above, children are not only sources of responses; they are also sources of organismic stimuli. A part of the child's environment is within the body. A child may get hit with a baseball, or feel a sharp stomach pain from excessive gas. Both are aversive stimuli; their strengths are analyzed according to their disruptive effect on whatever had been going on at that time. The methodological difference between the aversive stimulation of being hit by a ball and of stomach gas is not that one originates in the external environment and the other in the internal environment, but that the hit can be observed directly. The stomach pain must be "observed" indirectly with the aid of instruments or inferred from past observable interactions, such as what kind of food was recently eaten, state of health at the time of eating the food, and the like.

The example above refers to internal stimuli generated by a child's biological structure and functioning. There is another class of internal stimuli that is generated by a child's own behavior. Some of these stimuli originate in fine striped-muscle activity (such as in speech) and some in gross striped-muscle movement (such as in the regular alternation of leg responses, each stimulated by the other, in pedalling a bicycle).

All stimuli, whether generated by children's physiological functioning or by their own behavior, may acquire functional properties. That is, some stimuli may produce respondent behavior; some may strengthen, weaken, or signal operant behavior; and some may serve as setting conditions. Children thus produce stimuli that affect their own behaviors, just as stimuli that originate from the external environment influence their behavior.

In summary, children are clusters of interrelated operant and respondent behaviors and sources of stimuli that acquire specific functional properties for these behaviors. Some of these stimuli originate in the physiological functioning of children and some in their behaviors toward objects, people, and themselves. It is essential at this point to remember that much of children's behaviors change their physical environment and provide social stimulation to other people, and that the largest proportion of the stimuli that affect their behavior originates outside their bodies. A more comprehensive discussion of stimuli from internal and external sources follows.

THE ENVIRONMENT

Thus far we have described the environment in terms of *specific stimulus events:* physical, chemical, organismic, and social and have stated that these events, whether from external or internal sources, can be measured by the instruments of physics and chemistry, and/or by changes in the behavior of an individual. The environment also consists of *setting events,* or settings in which interactions occur (Kantor and Smith, 1975, pp. 46-47). An elaboration of the two components of the environment follows.

Specific Stimulus Events

Specific stimulus events may be divided into the following four convenient categories to help the reader understand the range and diversity of stimulation that must be taken into account in analyzing an interaction.

1. Physical: artifacts and natural phenomena—e.g., eating utensils, tools, tables, chairs, houses, roads, buildings, airplanes, rocks, mountains, trees, etc.
2. Chemical: gases that have an effect at a distance—e.g., the aroma of roast turkey, perfume, smoke, etc. and solutions in contact with the skin—e.g., acid, soap, antiseptic ointment, etc.
3. Organismic: the organism's own biological structure and physiological functioning or stimulation from the respiratory, alimentary, cardiovascular, endocrine, nervous, and muscle-skeletal systems of the body, and the organism's own behavior—e.g., stimulation from manual manipulation, balancing, moving about, and talking.
4. Social: the appearance, action, and interaction of people (and animals)—e.g., mothers, fathers, siblings, teachers, friends, strangers, coaches, policemen, pets, etc.

Remember that all the above stimuli may be analyzed in terms of their physical dimensions. In casual conversation, we refer to stimuli according to their physical characteristics. When asked to give an example of a stimulus, most people would very likely describe something in physical terms (e.g., "a red light," "a loud noise"). The fields of chemistry and physics have developed precise techniques for measuring and describing the physical properties of stimuli, notably by their weight, mass, length, wavelength, intensity, etc. When we use such descriptive measures, we are specifying the physical properties of a stimulus.

The functional aspect of a stimulus, or stimulus function. As we have stated, all the classes of stimuli listed above may also be measured by *changes in the behavior of an individual.* Suppose we invite a five-year-old into a dimly lit room (say 50-foot candles) in which there are a small table and chair. On the table are three attractive toys: an automobile, a doll, and an airplane. We observe the girl through a one-way screen for a few minutes and then suddenly increase the level of illumination twentyfold. The abrupt change in the environment is immediately noted by (1) the change in the reading of a light meter, and (2) the change in the behavior of the child. If the increase in illumination is consistently correlated with an observable change in her behavior, we may state a relationship between the two. Such data allow us to identify and classify the behavior changes: for example, closing the eyes or leaving the room when the light is too bright; or taking the toy auto to the light source to examine it when the light is dim. We can now be more specific about the relationship between the stimulus changes and the behavior changes. We can say that the stimuli have a certain functional relationship to the behaviors. The increase in light intensity elicits reflex behavior: a constriction of the pupil of the eye. When the light is bright, it marks the occasion for any response that decreases this stimulation, thereby strengthening the response (hence closing the eyes or leaving the room). When the light is dim, the situation calls for responses that maximize the light, so the child takes the toy close to the light to look at its details.

When an individual's behavior indicates that there is a functional relationship between a stimulus and a response, we can talk about the *stimulus function* in that relationship. Three kinds of stimulus functions are to be noted in the above example: (1) an eliciting function (the bright light is related to the constriction of the eye's pupil), (2) a reinforcing function (the bright light is also related to strengthening the response by closing the eyes or leaving the room), and (3) a discriminative or cue function (the dim light is a signal for the child to take the toy close to the light). We see then that a single stimulus may have more than one stimulus function (this is generally the case), and that stimulus function is simply a label indicating what the specific action of the stimulus is for an individual. Does it act on the class of responses preceding it, or on the class of responses following it? Does its action depend on the individual's history with similar stimulation in the past? And so on.

The concept of stimulus function has been introduced because it is important to distinguish between stimuli that have functions for an individual, in varying degrees of strength, and stimuli that do not. We say that a stimulus is any physical, chemical, organismic, or social event that can be measured, either directly or by instruments. But not all of these stimuli will have stimulus functions, that is, not all of them will have an effect on an individual's behavior. Consider a frown on the face of a parent. To a baby only a few weeks old, the frown could be a stimulus (he can see fairly well at that age), but it probably has no stimulus function: the baby's behavior is generally not apt to change reliably as a consequence of this stimulation. However, as he develops psychologically, this stimulus will acquire functions: first, like almost any other "face" the parent might make, the parental frown may produce giggles and smiles fairly reliably; later, after some experience with the punishment that often follows a frown, it may produce sudden halts in his ongoing behavior, followed by sobbing or crying. Hence, the significance of this special stimulus lies less in its physical composition than in the nature and strength of its stimulus functions, developed as a consequence of an interactional history.

There is another, and perhaps more important, analytical advantage to the stimulus-function concept. If we consider the environment of a child in terms of the functions of stimulus events, we shortcircuit some cumbersome and fruitless terminology because stimulus functions concentrate simply and objectively on the ways in which stimuli relate to behavior, that is, whether they elicit behavior, contingently strengthen or weaken it, signal occasions for its proper occurrence or nonoccurrence, etc. To understand the psychological development of a child, we need to describe and predict these kinds of relationships. And stimulus function is precisely the kind of concept that can bring order and meaning to the tremendous variety of stimulus events that make up an individual's world. In effect, the stimulus-function concept is an invitation to group together many diverse events into a few functional categories. A rejecting mother, a spanking, a fall from a bike, an aggressive sibling, a failing grade, lecturing a misbehaving child, a traffic citation, a snub—these and multitudes of others like them—may be regarded as having a common stimulus function: they are all stimulus events that weaken (punish) the behaviors that precede them. An affectionate mother, a pat on the head, a piece of candy, a ride in the country, a smile, an "A" in a psychology course, an enthusiastic "Good!" a window sign saying 'We gave," a handshake—these and many similar events—have another common stimulus function: they are all stimulus events that strengthen (reinforce) the behaviors that precede them. We must also consider other kinds of events, such as a mother's question, "What are you doing?" and the response "Oh, just putting my toys back on the shelf" will probably result in, "That's a good girl!'' (whose stimulus function is to strengthen the response that precedes it). On the other hand, the response "Oh, I'm just drawing pictures" (that turn out to be on the wall) will probably result in a spanking (whose dual stimulus functions are to weaken the response that precedes it and strengthen the response that avoids it—like telling a lie instead). The response "Oh, nothing" may result in a noncommittal grunt from a busy parent, which may have no stimulus function at all for the child and produces no change in his behavior.

The classification of environmental events into stimulus functions provides an organization of the conditions that control development, eliminating the need for subjective terms. Child psychology, as well as psychology in general, has been burdened with scores of terms meant to describe and explain a particular interaction. Too often, they are unobjective and impossible to apply to behavior in general. Witness the innumerable attempts to type parents into largely nonfunctional categories such as rejecting, indulgent, dominating, democratic, autocratic, etc. By replacing such typologies with a classification of stimulus functions, we concentrate instead on the kinds of stimuli a parent may provide and their function in strengthening, weakening, or maintaining some of a child's behaviors while leaving others unaffected.

The concept of stimulus class. Just as we showed earlier that responses always come in response classes, it is important now that we point out that stimuli also invariably occur in *stimulus classes.* For one thing, the environment rarely presents a stimulus to us in exactly the same way, time after time. Careful measurement of the stimulus and its components will show variation from occasion to occasion. A mother's face has a fair constancy to it, we may think, in that we know our mother's face from anyone else's face. But careful observations show that it is sometimes shiny, sometimes dusty, sometimes wet; occasionally creased into its facial lines, but sometimes smooth; the eyes range between fully open and fully closed, and assume a wide range of angles of regard; sometimes hairs fall in front of the face, sometimes not. Then let us remember that whenever we speak of a stimulus, we will almost surely mean a class of stimuli. Parallel to the definition of response class (page 20), the definition of stimulus class is a collection of stimuli that vary with the same behaviors (or behavior classes). Often, the members of a stimulus class will resemble one another in their physical attributes; sometimes they will be quite dissimilar in all but their effect on behavior. Thus, a child may be frightened of such diverse events as lightning, frowns, fast-moving vehicles, and high winds. However, they belong to the same class, because they evoke a fear response from the child.

Setting Events

So much for specific setting events as the first category of environmental conditions. We turn now to the second category: *setting context* or *setting in which a stimulus-response interactional sequence occurs.* A setting event influences an interactional sequence by altering the strengths and characteristics of the particular stimulus and response functions involved in an interaction. For example, a mother who routinely puts her eighteen-month-old son in a playpen after his afternoon nap finds that during the next hour the baby plays with his toys, tries some gymnastics on the side of the pen, engages in vigorous vocal play, and does not fuss at all. Consequently, the mother has free time for an extra cup of tea and a few telephone calls. One day, however, the baby is kept awake during his entire nap time by the unusual and persistent noise of a power mower on the lawn outside the bedroom window. When his mother puts him in the playpen this time (in the setting event or context of sleep deprivation), he whimpers, cries, is generally fussy, and does not play.

The analysis of the environment into specific stimulus event classes and setting events in this example is: first, the playpen and its contents are specific stimuli classes that set an occasion for playing. But this is true only if the child has previously had a nap, that is, only under the setting event of being "well rested." If the bed-sleep interaction has been prevented, having been replaced by the mower-awake interaction, then the child's response to the playpen is no longer playing, but fussing. It follows, therefore, that the bed-sleep interaction is a necessary precondition for the playpen-play interaction that succeeds it.

Let us elaborate on the concepts of deprivation and satiation of reinforcing stimuli as setting events. Food is generally considered a primary reinforcer (one that is not acquired through learning). Yet there are obvious times when food will not have a reinforcing function—just after a large meal or after a stomach upset, for example. There are other stimuli with primary reinforcing properties (e.g., water, sunlight), the effectiveness of which vary as a function of many things, one of them again being how much of the reinforcer the individual has had recently.

We can now state a formal principle: the reinforcing property of many (not all) stimuli depends on their supply or availability to the individual *over an extended period.* The prolonged absence of such stimuli is said to be a state of deprivation. The effect of such deprivation is to increase the reinforcing strengths of some stimuli. In contrast, the consumption of a large amount of a reinforcer is called satiation. The mark of complete satiation is the failure of a stimulus with a previously demonstrated reinforcing function to strengthen behavior.

The effectiveness of many reinforcers, the unlearned or primary as well as the learned or acquired kind, is, in all probability, subject to the effects of deprivation or satiation. Furthermore, we expect that different reinforcers will show differential sensitivity to deprivation-satiation occurrences for different children. The only way that we can be sure that deprivation and satiation procedures will have an effect is by making the proper tests on each stimulus which we are studying.

A setting event of particular significance in child rearing is the use of verbal instructions, saying, for example, "Now be a good boy while Mommy is shopping." Such a setting event may change a child's behavior for some time afterwards, in the sense that some "good" behaviors increase and some "bad" behaviors decrease. Or, a child left with a neighbor may play happily for a few hours if told "Mommy will be back for you soon," but may remain uneasy during her entire absence if his mother fails to establish this setting event by some reassuring remark, especially if the child has only a scanty history of being left with neighbors. In fact, children's histories of past interactions with their environments may be looked on as a collection of setting events (and specific stimulus-response functions) that influence their current behavior. Although a setting event can indeed by analyzed into its component stimulus events, it has been treated as a separate concept here merely because it is a convenient way of showing how the various aspects of the environment interact with behavior.

The following is a fairly comprehensive list of setting events grouped on the basis of the origin:

1. *Physical and chemical*
    a. Dark vs. light setting
    b. Land vs. water setting
    c. Wet vs. dry setting
    d. Extreme temperatures changes (desert temperature vs. snow-and-ice cold weather)
    e. Extreme noise-level changes (sound-controlled chamber vs. a boiler factory)

    f. Immediate physical background
    g. Clear, clean air vs. a heavy smog setting

2. *Organismic or biological*
    a. Satiation and deprivation of food, water, air, sexual activity, sunlight, etc.
    b. Behavior dispositions (high and low probabilities of behaviors) following an emotional interaction (e.g., "anger" behaviors after a gross insult or "joy" behaviors after the receipt of an extravagant gift)
    c. Drugs, especially depressants and stimulants
    d. Physical injuries, diseases, and illnesses
    e. Physiological cycles: diurnal, sleep, fatigue, and menstrual

3. *Social or cultural*
    a. Cultural situations: home, school, classroom, church, playground, hospital, theatre, neighborhood, and town
    b. The presence of an individual not directly involved in an interaction with positive reinforcing or aversive properties
    c. Instructions intended to guide behavior in a situation ("Be careful when playing in the water" or "Your father's in a bad mood today.")
    d. Attitudes: positive and negative

The three categories of setting factors combine in all sorts of ways in everyday situations. For example, a school principal (with aversive properties for a target child) may be present when the teacher gives verbal instructions ("Behave as a responsible citizen.") in a cultural situation (classroom). Here, the three setting factors—presence of person with aversive properties, instruction on how to behave in a class of situations, and the classroom—change all the stimulus and response functions in aversive ways. In other situations, the multiple setting factors change stimulus and response functions in incompatible ways, in which case those behaviors controlled by the stronger or strongest factors have zero strength (organismic setting factors of zero strength are similar to the biologist's concept of homeostasis or equilibrium) and the responses controlled by physical, chemical, and social settings dominate. For example, zero strength organismic setting factors together with appropriate physical and social settings increase the probability of exploratory and play behaviors of the young child (Bijou, 1976).

THE CONTINUOUS AND RECIPROCAL INTERACTION BETWEEN
THE CHILD AND THE ENVIRONMENT

The interaction between the child and the environment is continuous, reciprocal, and interdependent. In this approach, we cannot analyze a child without reference to an environment, nor is it possible to analyze an environment without reference to a child. The two form an inseparable unit consisting of an interrelated set of variables, or an interactional field, which is the subject matter of analysis.

In this formulation, the child is not a passive individual, one who waits to be stimulated by the environment; nor is he looked upon as a seeker of stimulation. Conceptualizing a child either as a receiver or an instigator of stimulation considers only the physical aspect of the environment and ignores the functional aspect. A child is viewed here as a cluster of interrelated behavior functions and a source of stimulus functions. The other source of stimulus functions is, of course, the external environment. All variables interact mutually, resulting in changes in both the behavior of the child and the functional nature of the environment. Sometimes the changes are subtle; sometimes they are dramatic. Sometimes they fluctuate between retardation and acceleration; most of the time they are progressive.

To understand these progressive changes, we analyze the interrelationships occurring during the span of development. We analyze one episode at a time. The one selected for study (usually dictated by a scientific or practical problem) always takes into account the relationships among (1) response functions, (2) stimulus functions, and (3) setting events. A simple episode such as a reflex interaction is analyzed as a sequence with a single functional phase (time frame) involving a setting event, an antecedent stimulus function, and a response function. (A person is strolling in the park and reacts to a sudden loud blast from behind with a startle response.) A complex episode such as responding to a question ("Where is the capital of the United States?") is analyzed as a sequence with several functional phases: an initial attending interaction followed by a perceiving or conceptualizing interaction, and ending in an affecting interaction ("In the District of Columbia.") Our exposition proceeds from simple to complex interactions, beginning with respondent or reflex behavior (Chapter 4) and ending with conflict, decision making, emotional and affective interaction, self-management, biofeedback, problem-solving, and creative behavior (Chapter 11).

DIVIDING DEVELOPMENT INTO STAGES

We have said behavioral psychology is concerned with an analysis of the interaction between past and present environmental events and responses. Considering that a child is always interacting dynamically with his environment, how can an investigator determine what is related to what? The answer is that an experimenter recognizes that there is continual interaction but assumes that no significant changes in conditions take place in the interactional unit selected for study. The unit he selects may be small, requiring only a fraction of a second, or it may be large, covering several months or years, depending on the specific plan of analysis that the problem seems to require.

In studying the influences of past interactions on currently observed behavior, it is convenient to divide the developmental stream into stages, and to investigate (1) the interactions within each, and (2) the continuities and discontinuities in behavior between successive stages. What, then, is the best way to divide the developmental cycle? Many have attempted an answer (including Shakespeare, who proposed seven periods or ages). Some psychologists, such as Gesell (1954) and Hurlock (1977), have divided the life span according to chronological age and refer to the behavior of the two-year olds, the three-year olds, etc. Others, such as Freud (1949) and Erikson (1963), have divided development on the basis of a personality theory and refer to the oral, anal, phallic, and latency stages. Still others, such as Piaget (1970), have divided development into intellectual phases: sensori-motor, preoperational, concrete operational, and formal operational. Stages by ages has the virtue of simplicity and objectivity, but is much too arbitrary to be helpful to anyone searching for relationships within and between successive periods. Significant interactions are not synchronized with the ticking of a clock. Basing stages on a personality or intellectual theory is an alluring prospect, but we do not yet have a comprehensive, empirically-based model of personality or intellectual development to serve as a reliable guide for stage segmentation.

Eliminating chronological age and personality or intellectual theory as inappropriate ways of dividing the life cycle, particularly for the early years, we are left with two alternatives. One is to mark the beginning and end of each stage by observable criteria based on behavior manifestations, social events, and biological maturation. To illustrate, infancy would be the period from birth to the onset of verbal language (behavior manifestation); childhood, the period from entering the first grade in school (social event) to the onset of sexual maturity (biological maturation);

and adolescence, the period from sexual maturity (biological maturation) to the age for voting (social event). (And voting, we should recall, was recently extended to 18-year-olds, at least partially according to the logic that if 18-year-old males are committed to a military service that proves increasingly deadly, in justice they should also vote in the same society that declared those wars. This may be a case of one interaction—military service at great risk—determining another—voting—so as to redefine a "stage." It is not frivolous to suggest that psychological development can be hurried, slowed, or otherwise determined by the political decisions of its society.)

The other alternative is to identify the developmental stages in terms of the major kinds of interactions that occur. We have opted for the second choice because of of its functional nature and shall use the terms and categories suggested by Kantor (1959). A brief sketch of the stages will display the general scheme.

Kantor suggests three major stages: foundational (or universal), basic, and societal. The foundational stage is that period of development when the organism is behaving as a unified system—as an organism—but is tightly limited by its organismic characteristics. Thus, most interactions initially are reflexive (or respondent, as Chapter 4 will define them), begin prenatally, and are highly uniform among individuals. Together with these reflexes are uncoordinated movements not yet tied to functional environmental stimuli. They seem to be related to organismic stimuli. Inevitably, these movements will confront the environment in such ways that they will become coordinated, efficient, and useful in relating to the invariable characteristics of that environment, such as the skill of touching, holding, and moving things. In their myriad ways, they will constitute the baby's repertory of abilities and knowledge. Out of them will emerge seemingly systematic attempts to explore more of that environment, attempts seemingly reinforced simply by the interactional characteristics of objects (including the physical properties of people) in the infant's world. This behavior is called ecological, by virtue of that fact; it is behavior that integrates the infant to the environment and begins to make the environment responsive to the infant, thus constituting the interaction so basic to Kantor's analysis (and ours). Clearly, then, this stage is well termed foundational; it describes interactions that may vary in degree and detail from one infant to another, but will be similar in form for all infants.

Growth interacting with such experience will presently yield a baby who is much freer from the early biological limitations, one whose nervous system is complete, whose muscles are strong, who needs less sleep and behaves vigorously for longer periods of time between feedings, and who can use that time and energy in manipulation, use, and exploration of the environment. Now the child will encounter experiences that are not uniform for all children, and those experiences will begin to accomplish the individualized teachings that will give each child unique, distinctive, personal attributes. Nevertheless, the exploratory, skill-developing and knowledge-developing interactions begun in the foundational stage will continue and become elaborated. They will also diversify as a function of individual experiences. Call this stage basic, then, especially in recognition of its necessity for what will follow.

And what will follow will be a development of skills sufficient to give us, the child's adult audience, an appreciation of each one as a capable, rational, manageable, open, and curious individual who obviously needs systematic instruction in the ways of our society: in reading, figuring, and all the other complex symbolic skills and in the accomplishments of our society and our culture. Thus, we expose our children to social agencies of development, most notably schools, but also neighbors, church groups, play groups, activity groups, the community's various parts, etc. This deliberate exposure to societal instruction and control will continue, at first by us and later by the children themselves, throughout their adult years. Clearly, then, these are societal interactions, and this is the long and complicated societal stage.

Thus, this analysis of behavioral development is a *stage theory;* its stages are periods during which most of the interactions have a certain consistent character. In general, it will be true that the foundational stage begins prenatally and continues until near the end of what is ordinarily called infancy; the basic stage begins then and continues until roughly school or preschool age; and the societal stage ordinarily will begin then and continue into adulthood. But these milestones are simple sociological accidents of our culture, and are not the essence of the stages. The stages are defined simply as the predominant character of the interactions going on at the time. Some children will spend more time in one; some less. (In particular, there will be considerable variation in the entering of the societal stage: many families foster their child's introduction to social institutions; others maintain closed, private nuclear family interactions virtually until the child must enter public school.) And of course, these stages do not begin and end abruptly. One fades into the next, so that there will be many times in a child's early life when the ongoing interactions seem as often to represent the earlier stage as the subsequent one. A developmental stage should never be used with calendar precision; it is a descriptive concept meant to be analytically useful, not restrictive or prescriptive.

SUMMARY

The child is conceptualized psychologically (1) as an interrelated set of behaviors that interacts with the environment, and (2) as a source of stimuli that is a part of that environment. The environment is defined functionally as events acting in relation to the child. Some of these events are classes of specific stimuli; some are classes of setting events. Reciprocal interaction between the individual's behavior and environment begins at conception and continues until death. The progressive change in children's interactions with their environments is their psychological development, and depends on the specific circumstances in those environments, past and present. The circumstances are classified as physical, chemical, organismic, and social stimuli, and are described in terms of both their physical and functional dimensions.

It should be apparent that this analysis of human development cannot in any way be considered the same as the behavior theory of John B. Watson (1930) who defined stimuli and responses only in terms of their physical dimensions and reduced psychological behavior to biological behavior. Nor can this analysis be identified with the learning theory of Robert R. Sears (1947, 1951) or the social learning theory of Bandura and Walters (1963) and Bandura (1977) because they include nonobservable hypothetical concepts modelled after the work of Hull (1943). But this formulation can readily be identified with the philosophy of science and behavior theory of B.F. Skinner and J.R. Kantor.

Our task now is to analyze the ways in which classes of behavior are initially related and then become conditionally related to classes of specific stimuli and setting events. We begin by analyzing simple respondent reflex interactions.

REFERENCES

BANDURA, A., *Social Learning Theory.* Englewood Cliffs, N.J.: Prentice-Hall, 1977.

BANDURA, A. AND WALTERS, R.H., *Social Learning and Personality Development.* New York: Holt, Rinehart, & Winston, 1963.

BIJOU, S. W., *Child Development: The Basic Stage of Early Childhood.* Englewood Cliffs, N.J.: Prentice-Hall, 1976.

ERIKSON, E., *Childhood and Society* (2nd ed.). New York: Norton, 1963.

FREUD, S., *Outline of Psychoanalysis.* New York: Norton, 1949.

GESELL, A., The ontogenesis of infant behavior. In L. Carmichael (Ed.), *Manual of Child Psychology* (2nd ed.). New York: Wiley, 1954, 335-373.

HULL, C.L., *Principles of Behavior: An Introduction of Behavior Theory.* New York: Appleton-Century-Crofts, 1943.

HURLOCK, E.B., *Child Development* (6th ed.). New York: McGraw-Hill, 1977.

KANTOR, J.R., *Interbehavioral Psychology* (2nd rev. ed.). Bloomington, Ind.: Principia Press, 1959.

KANTOR, J.R., *The Scientific Evolution of Psychology.* Vol. 1 & 2. Granville, Ohio: Principia, 1963, 1969.

KANTOR, J.R. AND SMITH, N.W., *The Science of Psychology: An Interbehavioral Survey.* Chicago, Illinois: Principia Press, 1975.

PIAGET, J., Piaget's theory. In P.H. Mussen (Ed.), *Carmichael's Manual of Child Psychology* (3rd ed.). Vol. 1. New York: Wiley, 1970, 703-732.

SEARS, R.R., Child Psychology. In W. Dennis (Ed.), *Current Trends in Psychology.* Pittsburgh: University of Pittsburgh Press, 1947, 50-74.

SEARS, R.R., A theoretical framework for personality and social behavior. *American Psychologist,* 1951, *6,* 476-483.

SKINNER, B.F., *The Behavior of Organisms.* Englewood Cliffs, N.J.: Prentice-Hall, 1938.

WATSON, J.B., *Behaviorism* (rev. ed.), Chicago: University of Chicago Press, 1930.

WINOKUR, S., *A Primer of Verbal Behavior: An Operant View.* Englewood Cliffs, N.J.: Prentice-Hall, 1976.

4

Respondent Interactions

Respondent interactions are often referred to as *involuntary behaviors.* In actuality, they represent a particular kind of high probability relationship between a stimulus class and a response class (Skinner, 1938). Unless an organism is physically prevented from responding or unless powerful setting events, such as extreme deprivation, strong emotional reaction, or excessive fatigue are factors, the respondent behavior will invariably follow an adequate stimulus. It is a temptation to believe that the organism is "built that way" through its phylogenetic history, that it has no "choice" but to act with its respondent equipment (Skinner, 1969, pp. 172-217).

Respondent behavior is not affected by consequent stimuli; they have a neutral function for this class of behavior. For example, reduction in the size of the pupil of the eye is respondent behavior. The contracting response invariably follows the presentation of a bright light to the open-eyed organism. Try standing in front of a mirror with a flashlight and watch how the size of your pupil changes as you shine the light into your eye. Next try to prevent the response; will yourself not to let your pupils contract. Your chances of success are near zero. For the fun of it, you might offer some friends $100 if their pupils don't contract when a light is flashed at an open eye. They won't be able to prevent the response when the eliciting stimulus is presented. Again, you might offer $100 if they can contract the pupils of their eyes without having a light flashed in. You won't have to pay off in either event. Now bet that you can do what has been impossible for them. (But be ready to pay off, just in case.[1]) We see, then, that respondent behavior is primarily the function of the

[1]On pages 115-116 we discuss some techniques which would allow you to win this bet. However, as you will have seen by then, this possibility does not abridge the statements made here about the insensitivity of respondent behavior to its stimulus consequence.

particular kind of stimulation that precedes it and of the appropriate setting event, and is not the function of the stimulation which follows it.

THE DEVELOPMENT OF NEW STIMULUS FUNCTIONS BY CORRELATING RESPONDENT BEHAVIOR WITH NEUTRAL ANTECEDENT STIMULI

People generally blush in a shameful situation. Blushing is a biological response: the dilation of the blood vessels in the face. This is one of a number of responses a human being is likely to show when, for some reason, he becomes excited. One reason for becoming excited is punishment. Children, when punished, typically blush (and may cry, and display many other responses, too). Generally, they are punished in situations that their parents define as shameful (that is, worthy of punishment), and we may observe that even as adults, they may blush when something reminds them of the punishment or when they are in similarly shameful situations. Yet they are not necessarily being punished on these occasions.

An analysis would proceed along these lines: blushing is one of a number of respondents elicited by punishment. Some of the characteristics of any stimulus situation that also includes punishment apparently come to elicit blushing, just as punishment does, simply because they have been associated with punishment in the child's experience. A young child may be punished by his parents for taking his clothes off and walking around naked, past a certain age of tolerance. In particular, parents are likely to punish a boy for exposing his genitals in public. Thus, in a certain culturally defined situation, exposure of the genitals is associated with a certain biologically powerful stimulus—physical punishment— which (among other things) elicits blushing. Later in life, a man may discover that he has been walking about with his trousers unzipped. He is likely to blush, especially if others are present. He has not been punished; he has been presented with a stimulus associated with punishment in his history. Clearly, this is a *conditioned* power. Without his particular history of punishment for this kind of exposure, the discovery that his pants have been unzipped would not activate blushing.

Similarly, food placed in one's mouth usually activates salivation, especially under mild food-deprivation. This is another example of a respondent. Because the sight of food is almost always associated with the stimulus of food in the mouth, the sight of food develops eliciting power for salivation. Had we usually been blindfolded before eating, the sight of food would probably not produce salivation because there would have been no history of associating the sight of food with the naturally effective eliciting stimulus of food in the mouth.

In accordance with our analysis of the interaction between the child and the environment (presented in the previous chapter), we can diagram the above example in three time-frames.

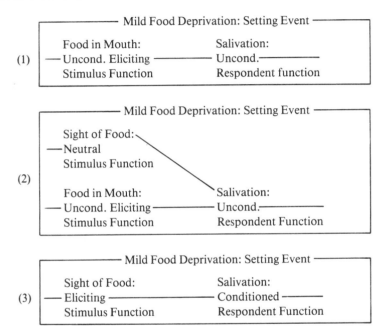

The first time-frame shows the relationship of the unconditioned eliciting stimulus (food in the mouth) and the response function (the salivary reaction) to food deprivation (the setting event). In this diagram, as well as in all diagrams that follow, the setting event is shown as a boundary line of the interaction to remind the reader that it influences *all* of the terms involved. The form of the boundary line is unimportant. We have presented it here as a rectangle. It could just as well be presented as a square, circle, or ellipse. The short line or lines before and after the first and last terms indicate that events occur before and after the episode isolated for analysis hence time is platted as going from left to right. All interactions in psychology are continuous. The second time-frame shows an instance of *pairing* a stimulus with a neutral function (sight of food) with the same unconditioned eliciting stimulus (food in the mouth) and the same unconditioned response function (salivary reaction). The third shows the change in stimulus function from a neutral stimulus function to a conditioned eliciting stimulus function: the sight of food now has the function of eliciting the salivary reaction. Note that at this point the response function, salivation, is designated as a conditioned respondent reaction.

The basic principle of respondent conditioning may be summed up thus: A stimulus that initially has no power to elicit respondent behavior may acquire such power, if, in the proper context, it is consistently associated (reinforced) with a stimulus that *does* have the power to elicit the respondent. This is an old formula of conditioning, dating back to the 1920's and the work of Pavlov (1927). It has been given a number of names since then, any of which you may meet in other readings in psychology: Pavlovian conditioning, classical conditioning, stimulus substitution, associative shifting, and type-S conditioning (S emphasizing the eliciting function of the antecedent stimulus). Respondent interactions, as you probably have gathered from the examples given, are largely restricted to those behaviors popularly called reflexes. (We prefer Skinner's technical usage of respondent to the other terms because we can state with precision what we mean by respondent. We would have considerable trouble sharpening the popular meaning of reflex.)

Two points must be understood about respondent conditioning. First, no new response is created in the conditioning process. Some of the features of the original response, as, for example, its strength, measured by its *magnitude* (or *amplitude*), *latency* (*time between stimulus and response*), or *duration,* may be altered, but basically it is a response that is a member of a class of responses that is linked with its appropriate eliciting stimulus. The responses an individual is capable of making are a function of his biological and genetic characteristics. The second point is that not all respondent behavior is conditionable. A tap on the patellar tendon accompanied by a tone has never, no matter how often the paired stimuli are repeated, produced the knee jerk in response to the tone alone. Respondent behaviors of this type are not included in this discussion. They are organismic (biological) phenomena, or neurological reflexes, the kind of responses a physician evaluates by tapping strategic spots with a triangular rubber-headed hammer and by scratching certain areas of the body.

THE ELIMINATION OF CONDITIONED RESPONDENT REACTIONS

What we have said is this: a stimulus that has been demonstrated to lack power to elicit a respondent reaction may be given such power by pairing it with a stimulus that has an eliciting function. The power so acquired may be weakened or eliminated simply by stopping the pairing, by repeatedly presenting the conditioned stimulus without the eliciting stimulus. When the conditioned stimulus is repeatedly presented alone, the respondent will be elicited at first but the reaction will finally disappear, so that the conditioned stimulus reverts to its original neutral state with respect to the respondent. We say that the conditioned respondent has now been *extinguished,* or deconditioned, or that the stimulus conditioned to bring it forth has been detached. For example, Watson and Raynor (1920) conditioned respondent crying in a nine-month-old infant by using the sight of a white laboratory rat as the conditioned eliciting stimulus. Their method was to pair the sight of the rat (which originally did not elicit crying) with a loud, sudden noise, which did elicit strong crying. After only five pairings of the sight of the rat and the loud noise (produced by striking a steel bar with a hammer), the presentation of the rat alone was sufficient to make the child cry. Later, after the rat had repeatedly been presented alone, the crying response grew successively weaker, its strength approaching closer to zero with each repeated exposure of the rat alone.

Mary Cover Jones (1924) varied this method so as to accelerate the detachment of a respondent from a conditioned eliciting stimulus. Working under Watson's direction with another child who had already been conditioned to cry at the sight of a rabbit (repeated presentation of the rabbit without any other stimulus that elicited crying), she presented the rabbit at a time when the child was eating candy. This association hastened the course of extinction, that is, crying in response to the rabbit decreased more quickly than by showing the rabbit alone.

Note that the dates of these studies were in the early 1920's. It is highly unlikely that they could be performed today. In recent years, largely under the impetus of public consciousness and explicit requirements of the United States Public Health Service, research conducted under federal auspices, or even in institutions that utilize federal funding and support for other purposes, must take into careful consideration the well-being and rights of all human participants. In many ways, only slightly less consideration is given for animal participants, except that animals may be sacrificed for sufficiently important potential knowledge gains. Prospective human subjects must be completely informed of the nature, purposes, and specific experiences scheduled for them, and they must be in full agreement before they are accepted for study. In the cases of humans not competent to agree (babies, retarded individuals, etc.) their legal guardians must agree. Review boards of disinterested but knowledgeable professionals (and, increasingly, nonprofessionals and sometimes persons identified as "advocates" of any special group to be studied) must study the research proposal and agree that no harm will result from its procedures before it can be undertaken. In our opinion, even if the Watson and Raynor study were to be proposed today, and it if had obtained the full, informed consent of the baby's parents, it probably would not secure the approval of the now-required review group. That group, we predict, would argue that babies should not be made to cry; that the establishment of a systematic fear of rats (and perhaps of other similar objects—see page 1) should not be added deliberately to the child's future problems; that the study had no obvious benefit for the child (even though it might benefit science to some degree) in that the child had no psychological problem that this study might improve or show how to improve; and that this study, proposed now, would add very little to what is already well-known about respondent conditioning processes.

But while we approve strongly of this probable action of the review committee, and of all similar actions by all similar committees, nevertheless we must point out that the last reason for disapproving the proposal—the fact that we already know about such mechanisms—is a result of earlier studies, including the Watson and Raynor study. The point is that the restriction of scientific research in the interests of never troubling a human subject is a costly one, in principle: there may be some experiments that would produce results so beneficial to all of us that they would be worth the trouble they caused their subjects. The value of current social policy in this regard is that research proposals are being evaluated in exactly this light—what are the risks versus the benefits?—and no matter what the answer, still cannot be performed without the fully informed consent of the subjects, the ones who must bear the trouble and thus most of all must agree that it may well be worth doing so.

An interesting sidelight: Fifty years after she had done this research, Mary Cover Jones was honored for her pioneering work in behavior therapy at the First Temple University Conference in Behavior Therapy and Behavior Modification. On that occasion, she presented an inspiring paper (1975) describing the early research of John B. Watson and related it to practices in modern behavior therapy.

GENERALIZATION AND DISCRIMINATION OF RESPONDENT INTERACTIONS

It is a fact of casual observation, and of repeated laboratory demonstrations, that conditioned respondent interactions may be elicited by stimuli other than those specifically involved in the conditioning process.

Recall the example of how Watson and Raynor taught a nine-month-old baby boy to cry at the sight of a white laboratory rat by accompanying its appearance with a loud sound. A loud noise typically elicits from an infant the unconditioned respondent interaction of crying. The boy's response to the white rat prior to the pairing was positive, consisting of approaching, reaching, and stroking responses. (Children do not fear rats unless they are taught to.) But after five pairings of sight and sound, his responses to the white rat, presented alone, changed to crying. This is simply a demonstration of respondent conditioning involving the same conditioned stimulus—the white rat. Subsequently, the investigators presented to the child, in succession, a rabbit, dog, sealskin coat, and a mass of white cotton. These objects were not previously paired with the loud noise, nor had they previously elicited crying. But they are all furry, white, or both, and now they all elicited crying. Elicitation of a respondent by stimuli that are merely *like* the one in the original pairing is termed a *respondent generalization interaction.* Research has demonstrated that the greater the resemblance the stronger the conditioned interaction.

In the same study, the investigators presented the baby with a set of wooden blocks. The baby did not cry; instead, he showed his usual manipulative behavior toward blocks. On the basis of the difference in the child's behavior in the two situations we may say that wooden blocks did not acquire generalized conditioned eliciting power (Watson & Raynor, 1920). In other words, he responded to objects resembling the white rat by crying, and to things not white and not furry (like blocks) with *other* behaviors. It would have been possible for the investigators to teach the child, through further, more specific conditionings and extinctions, to make discriminations among the objects that elicited respondent crying. To do this, they would have continued to pair the white rat and loud noise, and at the same time present one of the other objects, say the mass of white cotton, *without* the loud noise. After a sufficient number of contrasts, the child would be expected to show continued respondent reactions to the white rat, but not to the cotton. When this occurred, we would have said that the baby had learned a *respondent discrimination* reaction, that is, a previously generalized conditioned reaction had been refined and partly replaced by other responses, such as looking, touching, and babbling. Many of these interactions are not described as respondent, as we shall now see.

REFERENCES

Jones, M.C., A laboratory study of fear: The case of Peter. *Pedagogical Seminary,* 1924, *31,* 308-315.

JONES, M.C., A 1924 pioneer looks at behavior therapy. *Journal of Behavior Therapy and Experimental Psychiatry,* 1975, *6,* 181-187.

PAVLOV, I.P., *Conditioned Reflexes.* London: Oxford University Press, 1927.

SKINNER, B.F., *The Behavior of Organisms.* Englewood Cliffs, N.J.: Prentice-Hall, 1938.

SKINNER, B.F., *Contingencies of Reinforcement: A Theoretical Analysis.* Englewood Cliffs, N.J.: Prentice-Hall, 1969.

WATSON, J.B. AND RAYNOR, R.A., Conditioned emotional reactions. *Journal of Experimental Psychology,* 1920, *3,* 1-4.

5

Operant Interactions:
Behavior and Stimulus Consequences

From Chapter 4 we see that one of the ways in which progressive changes occur is through the interaction between the behavior of a child and antecedent stimulation. Another way is through consequent stimulation. The latter category is called operant interactions (Skinner, 1938). Some examples of operant interactions are: turning on a TV set results in a picture and sound; asking a friend for the time results in the reply, "It's two o'clock"; building a camp fire on a chilly evening results in warmth; removing a cinder from one's eye relieves the irritation; and turning off an alarm clock before it buzzes avoids a most irritating, aversive noise.

Trial-and-error behavior is one kind of operant interaction. When a class of operant behavior produces the goal object in a trial-and-error sequence, the occurrence of that event strengthens the tendency for the individual to make that response in similar situations. Such a tendency is called trial-and-error learning, and the response leading to the goal object is called the correct response. Another class of interactions involving operant interactions includes most of the behaviors that normative child psychologists (Hurlock, 1977) describe when they refer to children's motor, adaptive, language, or personal-social development. A third class of interactions with a heavy saturation of operant behaviors includes many of the classical categories of psychology such as attention, perception, cognition, volition, and concept formation. In Chapters 9, 10, and 11 we shall show how some of these terms are analyzed as part of complex interactional sequences.

Incidentally, operant behavior is sometimes referred to as voluntary behavior. This label is acceptable, and even helpful, in understanding a behavioral analysis of psychological development, provided no complicating implication of concepts such as the "will," "awareness," "consciousness," or "knowing" are injected into its meaning.

The fact that the strength of operant behavior depends largely on its past effects on the environment has been widely recognized and is exemplified by the descriptive statements in psychology that behavior is goal-directed, purposeful, or instrumental in achieving the organism's ends; behavior is adient (directed toward certain consequences); behavior is wish-fulfilling, or pleasure-seeking and pain-avoiding. All of these terms emphasize the belief that the results of behavior are essential for the understanding of the behavior. However, they may also imply that children actively seek or desire certain stimuli, and that they choose certain behaviors because those behaviors are likely to achieve their goals. Such implications are to be avoided. Therefore, we make an unequivocal statement *that operants are strengthened by stimulus consequences, those observed in the child's current situation, which includes the setting event, as well as those in the interactional history.*

FUNCTIONAL CLASSIFICATION OF STIMULI
IN OPERANT INTERACTIONS

Operant behavior produces consequences that may be grouped into three functional classes:

1. They may produce stimulus events that result in an increase in strength. These stimuli have the function of *positive reinforcers.*
2. They may remove, avoid, or terminate certain other stimulus events that result in an increase in strength. These stimuli have the function of *negative reinforcers.*
3. They may produce *or* remove still other stimuli that fail to strengthen an operant, whether the response produces these stimuli or removes them. Such stimuli have a *neutral function.*

The first class or group, stimuli that strengthen the operant behavior they follow, are called positive reinforcers because they operate when something is *added* to the situation, and are reinforcing because the behavior producing them or coincident with them is *strengthened.* Examples of positive reinforcers are milk (especially for a baby), candy (especially for a toddler), the approval of parents (especially for a young school child), the esteem of peers (especially for a teenager), and dollars from an employer (especially for an adult). The second group, stimuli that strengthen responses that remove, avoid, or terminate them, are called negative reinforcers because they operate when something is *taken away* from the situation, but still are called reinforcing because the behavior coincident with their removal is *strengthened.* Some negative reinforcers are: cold air (especially for an infant), a spanking (especially for a toddler), a frown from mother (especially for the young child), the ridicule of peers (especially for the teenager), and a ticket from a traffic policeman (especially for the adult).

We have found that students encountering this explanation of negative reinforcement tend to remember it incorrectly: negative reinforcement (probably because of the unpleasant nature of the stimuli involved in it, which we reduce, escape from, and avoid whenever we can) tends to be remembered as a punishment procedure—as a way of reducing the strength of a behavior. This is wrong. The stimuli involved in the negative reinforcement *can* be used to decrease behaviors, as you shall soon see—but that is not how they are defined as negative reinforcers. We suggest that you instruct your memory now that negative reinforcement is first of all a reinforcement operation, and that just as the word reinforcement implies, it is a response-*strengthening* procedure. It strengthens behaviors by allowing those behaviors to reduce, escape from, or avoid certain stimuli. Remember the nature of those stimuli: they are unpleasant. Then of course any behavior that reduces, escapes from, or avoids them will be strengthened. You may not like the process (neither do we), but you will learn new skills through it, not lose old ones. It is a behavior-strengthening procedure, albeit not one of the nicer ones.

We have been referring to addition and subtraction operations. Now is a good moment to introduce their proper technical names. These operations are called contingencies; when they involve reinforcers as stimulus *consequences,* they are called contingencies of reinforcement. A contingency in the most general sense is simply a statement of dependency, of the form "If A happens, then B will probably happen." The contingencies at issue here are of the form, "If a certain response occurs, a certain stimulus consequence will occur." Then there are two basic response contingencies: addition and subtraction contingencies. When a response class produces a stimulus, or increases the strength of a stimulus we shall call that an *addition contingency;* when a response class takes away, reduces, or avoids a stimulus we shall call that a *subtraction contingency.* These terms will figure again and again in the discussion to follow.

The third group of stimuli, those that do not affect the strength of responses they follow or are removed by, are neutral in that *neither an adding nor a subtracting operation* changes the probability of the usual level of the operant. Some examples are a frown for a new baby, or the epithet "sedulous!" for a typical ten-year-old. (In general, the older the child, the harder it is to find stimuli that are neutral. The reason for this will become apparent soon.)

How can we tell whether a particular stimulus (e.g., movement of the teacher's head in the direction of a child, offering a cracker to a preschool child, placing a young child in a room alone, offering a ride on a bike, or saying "Is that so?") will be a positive reinforcer, a negative reinforcer, or a neutral stimulus for a given child? There is no way of knowing[1] unless we make the following test. We observe some response class that is clearly an operant and that has a stable strength for a child. We then arrange conditions so that the stimulus class to be evaluated as a reinforcer is presented to the child consistently as a consequence of that particular response. (For example, each time a child says "Mar-mar," the thing or event, say a marble, is immediately given to him by the mother.) The strength of an operant class *before* the systematic application of reinforcement is called baseline rate or *operant level.* (An operant interaction cannot have a zero operant level or it could never be reinforced. In order for any operant interaction to be reinforced, it must occur at least once.) If the response class increases in strength over baseline rate or operant level (e.g., saying "Mar-mar" occurs more often), the marble is classified as a positive reinforcer. That is, the observation of this relationship (increased frequency of response due to the stimulus consequence) *defines* the stimulus class as one having the function of a positive reinforcer. No other kind of observation or judgment is necessary or sufficient.[2] By the same token, we may arrange the situation so that the operant behavior removes or avoids a stimulus. (For example, each time a child says "Cold" while in bed the mother immediately tucks in the blanket or puts on another blanket.) If the response class is strengthened under these conditions, that observation alone is necessary and sufficient to say

[1] In many instances we are able to make a guess because of what we know about the culture that the child shares. For example, we know that in our culture, saying "That's fine" when a child completes a performance will, for *most* children, strengthen the tendency to repeat the act under similar circumstances. We know, too, however, that it would be wrong to assume that saying "That's fine" will strengthen the preceding behavior for *all* children, and indeed, we may know some negativistic children for whom "That's fine" seems to be a negative reinforcer, not a positive one.

[2] In this discussion, we have ignored the important problem of making sure that the significant increase in response rate did not occur simply by chance, rather than as an effect of the new contingency between it and the stimulus being tested. That is, small children do say "Mar mar" at higher rates now, lower rates then, etc. We would conduct our test at a moment when for unknown reasons, that child is about to embark on a "Mar mar" splurge. (If you doubt that there are such splurges, ask any parent.) If we have any doubts about the cause-and-effect nature of the results of our test, we should simply repeat the test as often as seems necessary to make clear whether there is a systematic relationship or not.

that the stimulus class has the function of a negative reinforcer. Finally, if the operant class in either of these tests remains unaffected in strength, continuing at the usual stable level of strength that it showed before the test, the stimulus class is defined as neutral for that response class.

It should be pointed out that a stimulus class may be neutral for one response, yet reinforcing for another. A simple example will make this fact clear. Can we hire you to press a telegraph key for 25¢ per press? Probably so. Can we hire you to dig a ditch, 10 feet deep, 4 feet wide, and 100 feet long, for 25¢ per ditch? Probably not. (We hope not.) If we have guessed the correct answers, the 25-cent pieces fulfill the definition of positive reinforcer for you for key-pressing, *but not for ditch-digging.* This homely example will prove quite characteristic of reinforcers: they rarely have a universal function that never varies; instead, they have a reinforcing function for a given individual, for a given response, in a given situation. Thus there is no way to list the positive and negative reinforcers for people as a class, or even for any individual, without many qualifications. It is that diversity that makes up a great part of personality differences—and, in our opinion, that makes people much more interesting than would be the case otherwise. The practical problem of testing stimuli for their reinforcing value does not become a useless one, however. As a matter of practicality, choose a response to reinforce that does not require too much effort. The use of ditch-digging will suggest that most of us are impervious to any but a few very extreme stimuli as reinforcers, and that would indeed be a misleading conclusion. Most of us are sensitive to a great range of stimuli as reinforcers. (But it remains true that ditch-digging is not one of humankind's favorite hobbies.)

The importance of these three stimulus functions—positive reinforcer, negative reinforcer, and neutral stimulus—is so great in understanding child development that we offer the following algorithm in summary of the preceding discussion. An algorithm is a set of steps for accomplishing some goal. A cake recipe is an algorithm; the sequence of steps that you memorized in sixth grade for extracting the square root of a real number is an algorithm; etc. On the next page, we present a reinforcer-diagnosis algorithm.

THE STRENGTHENING AND WEAKENING OF OPERANT INTERACTIONS

We have been talking about the *strength* of an operant interaction. Let us clarify the term. In psychological work, as in everyday conversations, we measure or estimate the strength of a response in several ways. Dur-

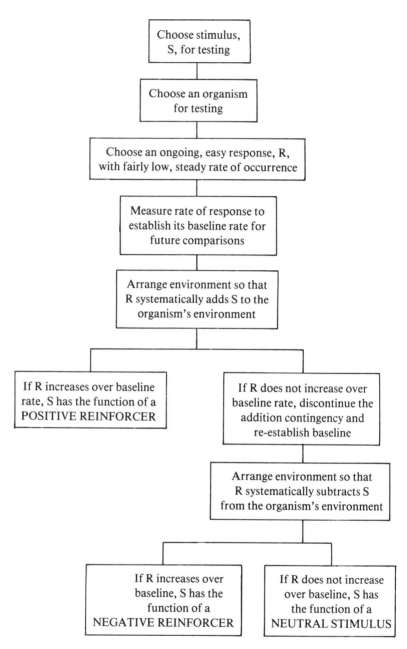

Figure 5–1

ing the past fifty years, it has been repeatedly demonstrated that one of the most useful measures of strength of behavior is the *rate* of occurrence: how often a member of a response class occurs within a designated unit of time under a specified set of conditions. In evaluating the behavior of children, the question we often ask first relates to its frequency of occurrence, for example, "How often does he suck his thumb, or whine, or have temper tantrums?" A second measure of the strength of a response is the *magnitude* (or *amplitude*) *of the response,* or the vigor with which it is performed, or the effort put into it. A child may whisper, speak in her usual voice, or shout "Go away" as increasing evidence of her anti-social behavior. A third measure of response strength is its *latency,* or the promptness with which it occurs with reference to a stimulus. The child who responds to a gift with a prompt "Thank you" is considered more polite than one who makes the same response sometime later (especially if a cue from a parent is necessary). When psychologists talk about response strength, they may be referring to any one of these measures or to some combination of them. Since these measures are not equivalent, it is essential to specify the measure used. Two studies dealing with some aspect of the relationship between, say, aggression and hunger may result in entirely different conclusions if one investigator measures the strength of aggressive behavior by the frequency of its occurrence, and the other by the usual magnitude of the occurrences.

The key fact is that we may regard the rate of a response, the magnitude of a response, and the latency of a response as three classes of responses, rather than as three aspects of the strength of the same response. The single most important reason for doing so is the fact that each of these aspects of response may be strengthened or weakened separately from one another simply by attaching appropriate reinforcement (or other contingencies) separately to each. For example: we may teach a young girl to say "Good morning" as she comes to the breakfast table. Suppose that we reinforce the rate by responding (with our delight, approval, and enthusiasm "Good morning to *you*!" or anything equally effective) every time she says "Good morning." We expect a high rate, at least once every morning. But magnitude and latency might be anything at all. Suppose we decide instead to reinforce only those greetings that are said loudly enough to be heard clearly by everyone at the table, but not those that are so loud that we consider them inappropriate or rude. Then we expect to produce well-modulated "Good mornings," but can have no firm expectations about their rate or their latencies. Or, we could choose to reinforce only those that were said no later than 15 seconds after she sits down. Then we should expect prompt "Good mornings," but can hardly predict how often, or how loudly, they will be said. We could, in the grip of precise social training ambitions, decide to try for a simultaneously high-rate, well-modulated, prompt "Good morning." Then we reinforce only those that are of proper volume and sufficient promptness; we reinforce every one that is so; and we may very well prompt these responses on any occasion when the girl is silent as she sits down. If one of us is deaf, we may reinforce only a loud, prompt "Good morning." If the girl responds to our rate-oriented reinforcers by repeating her "Good morning" after the first one, and we decide that only one "Good morning" per morning per group is appropriate, then we may reinforce the first "Good morning" but ignore all subsequent ones during that breakfast (unless, perhaps, someone else joins the breakfast group after the girl has come and made her greeting. Then we will reinforce *one* more "Good morning" by her to that person.) If we are a religious group, we may teach her to say "Good morning" only after she has said her personal grace. Or, we may not care how often she says it, or if she says it at all, so long as when she does say it, it is well modulated and prompt. Thus, we may have almost any combination of rate, magnitude, and latency within reason. It is as if these are three separate responses, each of which is available for learning. Hence, theories that predict something called "response strength" are doomed to trouble from the outset: the term is useful only as long as we remember that it is a chapter heading for the ways in which responses can occur, all of which are susceptible to specific, individualized strengthening and weakening procedures, separately from one another. However, since rate of response is the most useful and the one most generally under discussion, we shall usually mean rate in this text when we say strength.

We have pointed out that an operant response class may result in the presentation of a stimulus class or in the removal, avoidance, or termination of a stimulus class. We have also stated that the two kinds of stimulus consequences that can increase the strength of an operant are called positive and negative reinforcers. Keeping this terminology in mind, and disregarding the effect of neutral stimuli for the moment, we can see that an operant may have four kinds of consequences:

1. It may produce positive reinforcers.
2. It may remove, avoid, or terminate negative reinforcers.
3. It may produce negative reinforcers.
4. It may remove, avoid, or terminate positive reinforcers.

When the first consequence results in an increase in response strength, that defines the stimulus as a positive reinforcer. When the second consequence results in an increase in response strength, that defines the stimulus as a negative reinforcer. The outcome of the first and second arrangements is already known to us: whatever aspect of the response is systematically responsible for the stimulus consequence will be strengthened. We must already know that this is true; otherwise we would not have been able to label those stimuli as positive and negative reinforcers respectively. No doubt we have already been through the algorithm just described for stimulus function diagnosis. But knowing that a stimulus is a positive reinforcer tells us only what it will do in an addition contingency; it does not inform us what would happen if a response systematically *subtracted* that known positive reinforcer (the third arrangement above). Similarly, knowing that a stimulus is a negative reinforcer tells us only what it will do in a subtraction contingency; it does not inform us of what would happen if a response systematically *added* that known negative reinforcer (the fourth arrangement above). Repeated observations in experimentally controlled situations, with both animals and humans, produce a consistent answer: in each case the usual net effect is to weaken the response. We shall call both of these interactions "punishment." Thus, we have two techniques for strengthening (reinforcing) responses and two for weakening (punishing) responses. (We said earlier that the strengthening of a response is measured by an increase in its rate, an increase in its magnitude, or a decrease in its latency.)

What if the only thing we know about a stimulus' function is that it will accomplish punishment in an addition contingency, that is, it will weaken responses that add it to the environment? For the moment, we may call it a punishing stimulus, to index that function; and we should test its function in a subtraction contingency, to see if it is (as is usually the case) a negative reinforcer. But there are two possibilities: one is that we do not make this test of its negative reinforcing function, for some reason; the other is that we make the test but do not find results confirming that the stimulus is a negative reinforcer (possible, but rare). What then? In either case, continue to call the stimulus a punishing stimulus (because that is already clear); in the first case, bet (but do not insist) that the stimulus is also a negative reinforcer; and in the second case, bet (but do not insist) that another test, perhaps with an easier response, or in somehow better circumstances, would confirm the negative reinforcing function of this stimulus. Meanwhile, however, rest content with the label punishing stimulus—that is all that you *know*.

Similarly, suppose the only thing we know about a stimulus' function is that it will weaken a response class that subtracts it from the environment. Call this stimulus a punishing stimulus, and bet (but do not insist) that it will function as a positive reinforcer in an addition contingency. But do not call it a positive reinforcer until it passes the test of a positive reinforcer.

Now we can make a visual summary of what we have said so far about the ways in which a response class can have stimulus consequences, the effects of those various ways, and the names that should be attached to those effects. Such a resume is shown in Table 1.

Table 1 Operant Contingencies, Their Effects in Terms of Response and Stimulus Functions, and Their Technical and Common Names

Response Function	Effect on Behavior	Stimulus Function	Technical Names	Common Names
Adds a stimulus to the environment (addition contingency)	Strengthens	Positive reinforcer	Positive reinforcement	Earnings, reward, pay-off
	Weakens	Punishing stimulus (But try the stimulus in a subtraction contingency: it will usually prove to be a Negative Reinforcer)	Punishment	Hurt, spank, hit, scold
Subtracts a stimulus from the environment (subtraction contingency)	Strengthens	Negative reinforcer	Negative reinforcement	Relief, escape
	Weakens	Punishing stimulus (But try the stimulus in an addition contingency: it will usually prove to be a Positive Reinforcer)	Punishment	Loss, penalty, fine, cost, response cost

In Table 1, we have included some popular terms whose meanings often coincide with the precise meanings that these procedures now have in psychology. They are included only to help you understand the theory; because they often imply more than is intended, they are not used systematically in the text. "Reward," in particular, may be misleading. It often suggests a flavor of a child's conscious wishing for the reinforcer, a deliberate choosing of his responses in a judicious, rational manner, so that these responses seem likely to achieve the reinforcer. If this were the case, it would be reasonable to call the reinforcer a "goal," the operant response "purposeful," and the reinforcer a "reward." But we usually have no way of knowing whether this is so, and often it seems to be irrelevant—the reinforcer still reinforces (Rosenfeld and Baer, 1970). Remember that we must use these terms to explain the developing behavior of a child, from birth onward. Obviously, it would be inappropriate to apply these terms to newborn infants squealing helplessly in their cribs— terms that might suggest that they are consciously desiring certain goals and are deliberately seeking ways and means of achieving them. We will be closer to empirical facts (and further removed from mentalistic explanations) if we simply say, for example, "Milk has been tested and found to be a positive reinforcer under conditions of food deprivation; the operant responses by the infant that result in getting milk will tend to be strengthened, whereas operant responses that remove or lose milk will tend to be weakened." *This* summary of empirical relationships between certain operant response classes and stimulus consequences provides a good example of what we mean by a theoretical statement.

We have described the basic formulae of operant interactions by giving the essential characteristics of operant responses and the four ways in which they change in strength. All of these we might call examples of operant *conditioning,* that is, examples of ways of changing the strength of a response using reinforcers as consequences of that operant. Because the term conditioning often is restricted to those operations that *strengthen* responses, let us instead designate each of these four basic sequences as a "reinforcement" procedure. Let us say further that these four reinforcement procedures completely define the basic ways in which operant behaviors change as a consequence of reinforcing stimuli, and that all other procedures involved in the reinforcement of operant response classes are variations or combinations of these four.

We can describe operant conditioning as follows: a stimulus with the function of a positive reinforcer (e.g., custard) strengthens the preceding operant behavior (e.g., the child's bringing a spoonful of custard from a bowl to the mouth) in the context of a setting event (e.g., mild food deprivation). After a number of such response-stimulus coincidences, the operant response occurs smoothly and the rate of its occurrence is increased, that is, the child learns how to eat with a spoon.

The above description of simple operant conditioning can be diagrammed as follows:

```
┌─────────────── Mild Food Deprivation: Setting Event ───────────┐
│                                                                │
│   Bringing Spoonful of            Custard in Mouth:            │
│ ─ Custard to Mouth: ───────────── Positive Reinforcer ─────── │
│   Operant Response Function       Function                     │
└────────────────────────────────────────────────────────────────┘
```

THE WEAKENING OF OPERANT INTERACTIONS THROUGH NEUTRAL STIMULUS CONSEQUENCES

Now consider the effect of a stimulus class with a neutral function occurring as a consequence of a class of operant behavior. After members of a response class have been reinforced, what happens when the reinforcers cease, that is, when neutral stimuli now are the only consequences of a class of operants? We have already defined a neutral stimulus as one that does not strengthen the response of which it is a consequence. But what if that class of operants has been built up to considerable strength through previous reinforcing consequences, and then circumstances change so that the only results of the response are neutral stimuli?

A partial answer is that the interaction eventually will weaken. In fact, it will weaken until its strength is equal to what it was before it had been reinforced, or to its operant level. The weakening of an interaction by neutral stimulus consequences to its operant level is called *operant extinction*. When a class of operants has been weakened to its operant level and has stabilized there, it is said to be *extinguished*. We can diagram operant extinction, using the custard-eating example, in three time-frames.

Time-frame number 1 shows the operant interaction occurring above operant level. It is the same as the diagram showing operant strengthening. Time-frame number 2 shows that the reinforcing stimulus has been replaced by a neutral stimulus. It is the beginning of the extinction process. Time-frame number 3 shows that after repeated neutral stimulus consequences, the rate of operant interactions has returned to baseline.

This account is only a partial answer to the question of what happens when operant behavior is no longer reinforced. Other behaviors show

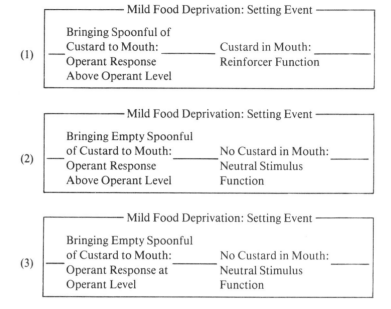

changes, too. Some of these are respondents of a kind usually called emotion (e.g., frustration); some are operants that in the past have been successful in producing the same reinforcer. (Variations in the form of the operants during extinction are frequently interpreted as "trying to figure out what went wrong.") It should be apparent even at this point in our exposition that operant and respondent behaviors interact in most forms of human interactions.

Extinction obviously is similar to punishment in that its effect is to weaken the operant (reduce its frequency of occurrences) to which it is applied. And there are two punishment procedures. Therefore, operant behavior may be weakened in three ways:

1. The response *produces* a negative reinforcer (punishment).
2. The response *loses* a positive reinforcer (punishment).
3. The response *produces* a neutral stimulus (extinction).

These three procedures, however, differ in certain essential respects. Extinction eventually returns response strength to operant level, but the two punishment procedures *may* weaken an operant well *below* its operant level. This raises a question parallel to the one that introduced this section of the chapter: What happens to an operant class weakened through punishment when it produces only neutral stimuli? In general, termination of the stimulus which follows operant behavior will result in the return to its operant level. This process of going from below operant level to operant level is sometimes called "recovery."

Thus, a neutral stimulus may be redefined in terms of operant level: a neutral stimulus is one that, whether produced or removed by an operant, fails to change the response strength from operant level, or fails to maintain it above or below operant level (if the response had been changed from its operant level by previous reinforcement or punishment).

At this point, the reader may ask about the case when a response has *no* stimulus consequences, neither reinforcing nor neutral. To the best of our imagination, there is no such case. Every response causes some kind of stimulus consequence. Calling some of them neutral means that they have no function for the organism in question, but they can have function for us, observing that organism, especially if we are watching with a question posed: "What are the consequences of that response?" Most responses rearrange some small part of the environment, and any response at least rearranges parts of the organism's body. There are nervous receptors that sense such body rearrangements. We tend to ignore many of these sensations, but they are there, as we discover if we care to attend to them; and a good deal of our behavior—especially our habitual motor skills—is in fact dependent on this stimulation for coordination. A familiar example is provided by the dentist who anesthetizes our mouth prior to potentially painful work. The anesthetization does not impair the physical structures necessary to our speech, yet while it lasts, our uniform reaction is that speech has become strange, even difficult. What we are testifying to is a change in the stimuli that arise within our mouth structures and muscles, and a change in the minute variations in these that occur with speech and help signal each successive part of each ongoing utterance.

Let us imagine a toddler, a girl, slightly over a year old, just learning to make a few recognizable verbal responses that her parents are more than willing to recognize as words. The girl's mother, we say, is fond of giving her sugar cookies, and usually says "Here's your cookie" when she hands one to the child. If we were to examine the child's verbal responses, we might find quite a number of syllabic responses, not otherwise recognizable as English words. One such response might be "Doo doo." This is a verbal sound, we find, that she makes about once or twice a day (its operant level). In general, it is received by the parents rather absent-mindedly, and, having no other stimulus consequences that are reinforcing, this response remains at its operant level. However, one day the mother happens to hear the girl saying "Doo doo," and for reasons of her own decides the child is asking for a cookie. With good will and warmth, she presents a cookie, saying "Here's your Doo doo!" After this, whenever she hears her child saying "Doo doo," she gives her a cookie together with a smile plus some obvious delight. Now, we discover that the strength of "Doo doo" is increasing: the child says it ten or twelve times a day, and on the occasions when she says it, keeps repeating it until it results in cookie-plus-smile-plus-delight, so that more and more often we hear her saying not simply "Doo doo," but "Doo doo, doo doo, doo doo, . . ." From these observations, it is clear that the response is being reinforced, perhaps by the cookie, or by mother's smile, or by her delight, or by all three. Thus we have an example of operant conditioning through the presentation of positive reinforcement for a particular response, "Doo doo."

But now the situation changes. Mother reads in the Sunday paper that a well-known dentist believes that too much sugar promotes tooth decay, especially in very young children. She is horrified to think that her practice of giving her daughter sugar cookies may be melting her teeth. The next time the child says "Doo doo," the mother neither smiles nor shows delight, nor does she give her a cookie. And from that point on, "Doo doo" is followed only by neutral stimulation, as it was before the mother decided that it meant "cookie." We shall probably observe that the child continues to say "Doo doo" for some time, but as occasion follows occasion when the response has been emitted and followed only by neutral stimulation, we shall see its strength falling until the response is back at operant level: once again the child says "Doo doo" only once or twice a day. And so we have an example of operant extinction.

But, you may say, this is not very realistic—the chances are that when the child asks for cookies the mother will not withhold her smiles, delight and cookies, but rather will tell the girl that cookies are not good for her, will console her, and may even suggest another activity to distract her. This may indeed happen. If it does, it is highly probable that "Doo doo" will take longer to weaken (if ever) because mother is now potentially reinforcing "Doo doo" with her attention, affection, or other social reinforcers.

There are several other points about operant conditioning to be gleaned from this example. For instance, it might be asked "Which of the three obvious stimulus consequences—cookie, smile, and delight—of this response reinforced saying 'Doo doo'?" We do not know, but we could find out by applying the definition of positive reinforcer to each. The mother might continue giving a cookie for the response, but would neither smile nor show her pleasure. If the strength of the operant is unaffected, we might conclude that the cookie was the critical reinforcer (or at least, *a* reinforcer). But we should also have the mother stop giving the cookie, yet continue to smile for the response, while withholding all signs of delight. And we should also have the mother continue to show delight, but withhold smiling and giving cookies. We might discover that any of these stimuli is effective in continuing "Doo doo" at its frequency, or that one is more effective than another, or that two in combination are more than twice as effective as either alone. The essential point here is a reiteration of what has already been said about reinforcers: only by testing can you tell what is an effective reinforcer for any individual. It is worth re-emphasizing that because of differences in individual interactional histories and the current stimulus situation, one child may be better reinforced by cookies, another by the mother's smile, and a third by her delight. There are relatively few reinforcers that will work for everyone; each child may be reinforced by a different list of stimuli. We can only make such a list by testing a very wide range of stimuli. And, indeed, we suggest that one of the most productive ways of accounting for the differences in personality that distinguish children is to list and rank the usually important reinforcers for each individual child.

A second point to note in the example is that *no new response was created by the reinforcement procedure;* an already existing response was strengthened. A response can be conditioned by reinforcing consequences but it must occur in order to have consequences. Operant conditioning does not produce new classes of responses; *it strengthens or weakens old ones, and puts them together in new combinations.* For example, we may take a young girl who does not play the piano, and after a few years of proper reinforcement produce reasonably creditable playing. We have not strengthened piano-playing from zero strength to a considerable positive value. Instead, we have separately reinforced a large number of already existing finger movements, strung them together in novel combinations, and established some standard time intervals between them (rhythm) through a long and complex series of strengthening (and weakening) procedures. We then label this chain of responses piano-playing as though it were a new response, but in fact, it is the *arrangement* that is new, not the responses that go into the arrangement.

If operant conditioning, like respondent conditioning, does not create new responses but instead merely strengthens, weakens and rearranges old ones, then where do the old responses come from? As we have said, the answer lies with the findings from the biologist, since this question has to do with the genetic and biological characteristics of the organism, his physiological structure and functioning. You will recall that in the introductory section, we discussed the relationship between animal biology and behavioral psychology and stated that behavioral psychology looks to the biological sciences for information about the physical equipment of an organism at various times in the developmental cycle. Certain responses exist; we study them in their interaction with environmental events. In the same way, astronomers account more readily for the behavior of stars than for the *facts* of stars; and chemists account for the behavior of elements but not for the elements themselves. The origin of stars and of chemical elements is the domain of other sciences.

A third point to be stressed in this example concerns the meaning that "Doo doo" may have for the child. All that the observer knows is that "Doo doo" is a verbal response that is reinforced by cookies. It does not follow that the child will name cookies "Doo doo" when she sees them, nor does it follow that she will think of cookies when she hears someone else say "Doo doo." It would even be inappropriate to say that she wants cookies when she makes this response. In general, we cannot attribute any significance to this child's response other than that we have observed an increase in the frequency of her saying "Doo doo" under certain historical and temporary circumstances. Our example gives us no special insights into the child's inner mental world, if such exists.

SHAPING

Although we do not know how to make responses, there is a practical technique that sometimes seems to do just that. It is called response induction, differentiation, successive approximation, or shaping. Properly speaking, this technique is simply a part of response generalization (to be discussed in Chapter 8); but it may be remarked on here because of its logical relevance to the preceding point (that operants are reinforced, not made).

In a now-famous clinical case representing an early application of behavioral logic to a serious behavior problem, Wolf, Risley, and Mees (1964) were attempting to save the visual capacity of a seriously misbehaving young boy who recently had undergone surgical removal of the lenses of his eyes because of cataracts. The child would not wear the eye-glasses that now were necessary to produce a focused pattern on his retinal cells (this was part of a generalized pattern of misbehavior constituting serious problems which threatened the child's future). Without consistent focused visual stimulation, the attending medical expert feared, the child's retinal cells might degenerate, causing irreversible organic blindness. Besides, without the glasses, he was functionally blind already. A reinforcement program was applied to glasses-wearing, but appeared to be useless because glasses-wearing never was observed to occur and thus could never be reinforced. Reacting to that momentary failure, the investigators applied the principle of response induction: they reinforced responses that were apparently related to glasses-wearing, even though they were not actually glasses-wearing. Thus, they reinforced for a while touching the glasses, which did occur sometimes. Touching the glasses soon increased the frequency; then, they reinforced moving the glasses in the air, which, now that the glasses were being touched so often, occurred with fair frequency. Glasses-waving soon became frequent, and in the process, some waves toward the child's face began to appear for the first time. Reinforcement was restricted exclusively then to glasses-waves that brought the glasses near the boy's face, and as that succeeded, occasional waves that brought the glasses to the face appeared for the first time, and these were reinforced exclusively. Proceeding in this way, the investigators were able to evoke successively closer approximations to the response that they desired as the final recipient of reinforcement, until glasses-wearing itself occurred. It was then reinforced exclusively, and stabilized at desirable levels of day-long usage. Fancifully, it might appear that the successive contingencies of reinforcement had carved a new response out of the old behavior patterns—and it is common in this field to refer to all such processes as "shaping" (or, less graphically, as successive approximation). Without in the least devaluing this most useful and critical technique, we point out that, nevertheless, on analysis it is a case of rearranging existing behaviors—getting the existing behaviors into novel arrangements by reinforcing *arrangements* of behaviors, or chains of behaviors, that are close to the desired but still absent behavior.

Shaping is one of the most useful clinical tools generated by the behavioral approach. It is essentially an exercise in response induction, or generalization (see page 83) combined with clinically directed response differentiation by a teacher or therapist. In the general case, a response class is desired that is totally absent. (In theory, that means that an arrangement or chain of presently existing responses is desired, but although the responses exist in the individual's repertory, that particular chain of them does not—recall the piano-playing example of page 58). Then a class of responses is selected for reinforcement that is present in the individual's present repertory and that has some resemblance, even a remote one, to the desired response. The remotely relevant response is reinforced; in its new strength, it will probably be associated with other equally new responses, which we recognize as the usual outcome of reinforcement. That phenomenon we have already learned to label response induction. In those new, generalized responses, we should be able to find one or several that are closer approximations to the final response desired —at least, some response or responses that are somewhat less remote than the originally reinforced response. If we can find such responses (and almost always, we can), we must also begin to reinforce them. We are looking for a moment when these new responses will have sufficient strength to occur reliably so that we can reinforce them exclusively and discontinue the reinforcement of the original response. As we do so, we expect response generalization to continue to occur—but now it is occurring from a new base, from the new responses now receiving exclusive reinforcement. Thus, we expect still newer responses to emerge presently, and some of these should be even closer to the desired response because the response from which they have generalized (the second target of reinforcement in our sequence so far) was itself closer to the desired response than was the first response. Then we can repeat the cycle, looking through those newer responses for a more suitable one to reinforce exclusively, choosing the moment to do so when it will have sufficient strength to prosper under exclusive reinforcement.

If we move too rapidly, the new target may increase in strength so slowly that much of the clinical value of the work will be jeopardized, and the child whose repertory we are trying to augment may become restless for lack of reinforcers. If this happens, we can always step back one cycle, choosing a more frequently occurring response to reinforce, even though it may be somewhat farther from the final desired response. It is more important to keep the child in a systematic training program than to jump immediately from new response to new response. And it has become a truism in the applied field that it is *always* possible to find a sequence of responses in which the later steps appear through generalization as their predecessors are strengthened that with reinforcement will end with the desired class of responses.

It may often be the case that we cannot predict what sequence of responses and their generalizations we shall follow to some desired final behavior. Experience with certain standard problems have led to equally standard expectations about the curriculum (program) to use; but with many problems, even familiar ones, a given individual may display different patterns of new-response generalizations than other individuals sequence of responses in which the later steps appear, through generalization, as their predecessors are strengthened and with further reinforcement will end with the desired class of responses.

This process may be visualized in the following time-frames. Suppose that we wish to develop the response R_{20} in an individual, but R_{20} never is seen and so cannot be reinforced. Instead, R_{10} is seen fairly often. These subscripts are meant to represent places on a continuum of resemblance, such that an R_{19} very closely resembles R_{20}, R_{18} less closely resembles R_{20} than does R_{19}, etc. Lacking any sufficiently high-rate response closer to the desired R_{20} than R_{10}, we reinforce R_{10}. The result should be an increase in the strength of R_{10}, of course, but also some generalization around R_{10}, such that examples of both R_9 and R_{11} appear fairly frequently, and with somewhat less frequency, examples of R_8 and R_{12} also appear. R_8 and R_9 are of no use to us; they are not on the way to R_{20}. But R_{11} and R_{12} are, R_{12} especially.

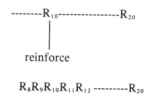

Therefore, we now shift our reinforcers to R_{12}, as soon as R_{12} seems sufficiently strong. (If necessary, reinforce both R_{10}, which is quite strong, *and* R_{12} until R_{12} strengthens. If for some reason R_{10} is easier to perform than R_{12}, this tactic may not work, and the reinforcement should be shifted to R_{11} instead, discontinuing the reinforcement of R_{10} as we do so.) The shift to R_{12}, and the results, are shown in the next two time-frames:

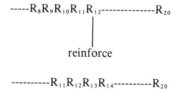

Thus, for lack of reinforcement near them, R_8 and R_9 have been extinguished, but R_{13} and R_{14} have now appeared, due to the reinforcement of their near neighbor, R_{12}. Then reinforcement may be shifted to R_{14} presently, as shown:

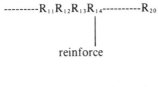

$$--------R_{11}R_{12}R_{13}R_{14}----------R_{20}$$

reinforce

with the result:

$$---------------R_{13}R_{14}R_{15}R_{16}----R_{20}$$

Thus, these steps can be continued until R_{20} appears, whereupon it can be reinforced, and eventually reinforced exclusively, and the problem is solved. Apparently, a new response has been created out of nowhere, or more, accurately, out of some already-present, remotely related response(s). But recall that upon close analysis, it will be seen that what has been created are some new arrangements or chains, labelled R_{20} for convenience, but in fact made up of already existent component responses.

We have not offered an explanation for response induction or generalization, only a description of it as a phenomenon and an indication of how it may be used in practical contexts. An explanation would be a matter of considerable guesswork at this time. An appealing set of guesses is to conceptualize any response that we deal with as actually composed of much smaller component responses. Reinforcing the large response, then, actually consists of reinforcing varying samples of its components, not all of which recur in the same way every time the larger response is given. (Think of the variety of ways in which you say "Hello" to others. We may call all of them the "Hello" response for convenience, but we can readily see that it has variations in components from time to time.) Then, by chance or through unknown quirks of past history, the reinforcement may favor not one arrangement of those components, but (much more likely) some number of them: now one, now another, so that we see a number of closely related "new" responses emerging, out of which we select the one we want for shaping.

This theoretical account has the virtue of being stated in terms that in principle could be subjected to objective experimentation. Unfortunately, the composition of some responses is not so easy to inspect as the composition of others, and when that it is true, the theory becomes an exercise in unobservable assumptions and beliefs. For that reason, we offer it as an example of a potential explanation, sometimes susceptible to experimental examination in a direct way, but nevertheless not yet to be relied on as the sole correct answer. Furthermore, we can readily believe that individuals could be taught to generalize in particular manners or styles, using algorithms for that purpose (see pages 86-89); thus, generalization is a phenomenon that probably encompasses a number of underlying mechanisms, rather than a single one. It is the direct development of these potential mechanisms that seems to us to be the important business of behavioral science, rather than their postulation in ways that explain but do not extend our ability to be useful.

REFERENCES

HURLOCK, E.G., *Child Development* (6th ed.). New York: McGraw-Hill, 1977.

ROSENFELD, H.M. AND BAER, D.M., Unbiased and unnoticed verbal conditioning: The double-agent robot procedure. *Journal of the Experimental Analysis of Behavior,* 1970, *14,* 99-105.

SKINNER, B.F., *The Behavior of Organisms.* Englewood Cliffs, N.J.: Prentice-Hall, 1938.

WOLF, M.M., RISLEY, T.R., AND MEES, H.L., Application of operant conditioning procedures to the behavior problems of an autistic child. *Behavior Research & Therapy,* 1964, *1,* 305-312.

6

The Role of Time
and Number of Contacts
in Acquisition of Operant
Interactions

In increasing the probability of occurrence of an operant interaction through reinforcement procedures, two conditions play critical roles. One is the *time* between the operant behavior and the consequent stimulus and the other is the previous *number* of contacts between the operant behavior and the consequent stimulus.

THE RELATIONSHIP BETWEEN OPERANT BEHAVIOR AND THE TIME OF ITS REINFORCEMENT

We have stated that operant behavior is sensitive to consequences. The *promptness* with which operant behavior is followed by consequences can be as important as the consequences themselves. Investigations have shown that, in general, the more immediately an operant class is reinforced, the more effectively its strength will be changed. In technical terms we refer to this relationship between time of reinforcement and increment in operant strength as the *temporal gradient of reinforcement.* Imagine a father coming home one night, tired from a hard day's work, and sinking into his favorite armchair with the newspaper. His wife, observing his general state of fatigue, calls their two-year-old son aside and says, "Timmy, please bring Daddy his slippers." Assuming that this is an intelligible suggestion to the child, he complies to please his mother. The very moment the youngster approaches his father with his slippers is critical. If his father immediately looks up from his paper, sees the child there with the slippers, and bursts out an obviously pleased "Well! What have we here?", and then hugs and thanks him, the slipper-fetching response will be greatly strengthened by this prompt reinforcement (if his father's delight is an effective reinforcing stimulus for the child, as we assume it no doubt is). As a consequence, it is probable that the next time the same act is appropriate (the next evening when the father again sinks into his chair to read his paper), the boy again will bring the slippers, perhaps without a suggestion from his mother. Again, if his father is punctual with his reinforcement, the response will be further strengthened and may become one of the household rituals.

Now consider the consequence of another interactional sequence. Suppose that on that first occasion, the father was so deeply engrossed in the news that he did not notice that the boy had brought the slippers. Discovering them several minutes later, he might say something nice about having his slippers brought to him, but by then the child might be playing with blocks in the middle of the floor. According to the temporal gradient of reinforcement, the response to profit most by the father's delayed reinforcement will be what the child is doing at the instant of the reinforcement, and that is block-stacking, not slipper-fetching. From the point of view of wanting to strengthen slipper-fetching, we are off to a bad start. The child is not likely to repeat the slipper-bringing operant the next time it may be proper to do so, unless the mother again suggests that he should. And if she does, the father had better be more prompt with his reinforcement, or the act may never become a part of the child's repertory.

Some observations on the effectiveness of prompt reinforcement illustrate the basic nature of the rule, "What behavior is strengthened is what is reinforced." Skinner (1972) trained pigeons to peck at a disc on the wall of a cage by reinforcing this response with a buzzing sound (which was reinforcing to the hungry pigeon because it had been associated with food—a principle we shall discuss presently). He showed that if the buzzer is presented even *one-twentieth of a second* after the pigeon has pecked at the disc, the pecking response will not be learned readily. Amazing? Let's see why this is so. When a pigeon pecks at a disc, the sequence of responses is very swift and precise, so precise that when the reinforcement arrives more than one-twentieth of a second after the pigeon's bill hits the disc, it is a closer consequence of the recoil of the pigeon's head from the disc than it is of the approach of its head toward the disc. Hence the backward motion of the head is reinforced more promptly than the forward motion, and what the pigeon begins to learn is to jerk its head *backward.* One might think that a normal pigeon would "see" what was involved in getting the reinforcement and would peck the disc accordingly. But investigations of learning seem to show more and more that it is less important what an organism can deduce from a set of experiences than what response was most promptly reinforced.

The reader should have a trenchant question ready at this point: how can the temporal gradient of reinforcement be so important in human behavior when most of the reinforcement contingencies that I undergo are not as precise as that, and yet I learn? And more to the point, I could have deduced that it was the key-peck that produced the reinforcer, not the head-back response. Part of the answer is in the next section (which, to summarize it perhaps too briefly here, shows that imprecise reinforcement contingencies can teach despite their imprecision, when, over many successive experiences, their only *consistent* relationship is between a certain response and the imprecisely delivered consequence). Part of the answer, however, is to acknowledge that you very probably could have deduced that it was key-peck, not head-back, that produced the consequence; and to inquire into the nature of that deduction and its relevance to your ability to learn and develop. Although the detailed treatment of such topics requires considerable presentation of fact, argument, and analysis, and therefore is taken up later in this volume (see pages 96–124), any presentation of theory should indicate how the process figures in developmental interactions. This is particularly true for a theoretical presentation such as this, which utilizes such concepts so very sparingly (and, indeed, reluctantly).

MUST THERE BE A CAUSAL RELATIONSHIP BETWEEN AN OPERANT AND ITS REINFORCER?

In the preceding section, we remarked that reinforcement best profited the response that most immediately preceded it—and in some of those examples, the immediately preceding response was not, in fact, the condition producing the reinforcer. In the case of the pigeon, the head-back response had no connection with the machinery that delivered food to the animal. Due to the stereotype of pigeons' pecking behavior, it was simply a response almost certain to occur immediately after the response (key-peck) that did activate the food machinery—and so, if the machinery were a little late in operation, it would be head-back that most immediately preceded that operation. Can behavior really be strengthened by reinforcers that the behavior does not cause? The answer is yes. The phenomenon is sometimes referred to as *adventitious reinforcement,* and hence as adventitious conditioning; sometimes, very daringly but also instructively, it is called superstitious conditioning. We might very well say that the unfortunate pigeon confronted with a slow food-delivery mechanism is likely to develop a superstition—that a head-back tic produces food. We know, of course, that it does not. But do we not know people who carry a charm (a rabbit's foot, classically) to bring them good luck? We know that the charm does not make the world work differently—

why don't our friends know the same thing? Indeed, they may say that of course they know that. Nevertheless, they will carry the token—perhaps it makes them feel better.

Why do superstitions survive the knowledge that they are not really true? In part, apparently, because reinforcement contingencies sometimes can be more effective than the algorithms that make up a part of knowledge; and in part, because a superstition can become a self-fulfilling prophecy. Suppose that we carry charms much of the time. It will be fairly simple for us to note all of the good fortune that occurs while we have the charm with us—that reinforces carrying it. It will also be simple to especially note the ills that befall us when we happen not to have it with us. That will punish us for leaving it behind. The algorithms that make up memory processes in this case can be used to emphasize accidental reinforcements as if they were indeed contingent on the presence of the charm; here is a case of an algorithm making reinforcement more potent than it ought to be. Furthermore, if we carry the charm constantly and especially if our life is much more positive than negative, it will be true, with or without the selective use of memory, that carrying the charm will encounter much reinforcement. This is reinforcement that would have happened anyway, of course, in the presence or in the absence of the charm. But the superstitious behavior guarantees that most of this reinforcement will be in the presence of the charm, and so carrying it will be reinforced as well as the other, truly antecedent behaviors that earned that reinforcement.

It should be apparent that this discussion assumes that a response need not be reinforced every time it occurs to profit from the reinforcement. That is true. The facts involved are well known, extensive, and very significant. They will be presented in a subsequent section of Chapter 7. But our discussion of the temporal gradient of reinforcement made it important to recognize the phenomenon of adventitious or superstitious conditioning at this point, and to establish it as an explanatory principle (and a readily observable, usable, and repairable one) in the analysis of much behavior that may seem strange, irrational, or simply inexplicable by the ordinary reinforcement contingencies of the world.

RELATIONSHIP BETWEEN THE STRENGTH
OF OPERANT BEHAVIOR AND THE NUMBER OF CONTACTS

The temporal gradient of reinforcement is an important principle, but equally important is another principle that explains why the relatively slow and imprecise reinforcement practices of parents, teachers, and peers succeed in developing children's behavior. This principle may be stated as follows: the strength of a class of operant behavior depends on the number of times it has been reinforced in the past, within limits. The more often it has produced positive reinforcers or the removal of negative reinforcers, the stronger it becomes; the more often it has produced negative reinforcers, neutral stimuli, or the removal of positive reinforcers, the weaker it becomes.

Let us re-examine the example of the pigeon in light of both the temporal gradient of reinforcement and the number of reinforcements. Every time the pigeon pecks at the disc, it makes two responses, "head-forward," followed by "head-back." If the reinforcement (the sound of the buzzer) arrives more than a twentieth of a second late, it follows both of these responses, and thus both are reinforced an equal *number* of times, but the "head-back" response is strengthened more than the "head-forward" response because it is more promptly reinforced. As a result, the pigeon does not learn to peck properly at the disc. We may apply the same two principles to the boy who brings slippers to his father. The boy may learn slowly because his father cannot apply his reinforcer (delight) as quickly as a mechanical instrument might reinforce a pigeon. Therefore, any response that happens to intervene between the arrival of the child with the slippers and his father's reinforcement will profit more from the reinforcement than will the slipper-fetching response. But in this example, we can see that the responses that intervene between slipper-fetching and reinforcement are likely to be different ones each time the child approaches his father: perhaps he will stand and look at his father, perhaps he will look at the slippers, perhaps he will say something, or perhaps he will pet the dog who happens by at that moment. In other words, we expect an inconsistent sample of behaviors to occur between the time the child arrives and the time father gives the reinforcement. In terms of the distribution of reinforcement, then, we see that it is the slipper-fetching response that is reinforced every time, however belatedly; the other responses are (each) reinforced, perhaps more immediately but usually less often and less consistently. Thus, if his father is not *too* slow in applying reinforcement, slipper-fetching eventually will be strengthened more than other responses because it is more consistently reinforced, and it will be learned and become a part of the child's social repertoire. The quicker the father is, the quicker the youngster will learn to bring his slippers. But if his father is *too* slow, there may well be no learning at all, even though the *consistently* reinforced response is slipper-fetching.

Much of the rate of a young child's learning may be related to the operation of these two principles: the temporal gradient of reinforcement and the number of reinforcements. Learning typically is fairly slow largely because of the delayed and imprecise reinforcement practices of parents and teachers. As in the example, learning may not take place at all simply because the reinforcers come too slowly, and the intervening responses manage to be reinforced better than the desired behavior. Nevertheless, the child learns (obviously), for imprecise as their reinforcement practices may be, parents and teachers are at least reasonably consistent and persistent in recognizing the particular behavior they wish to strengthen.

A discussion of the number of reinforcements and strength of an operant class would be incomplete without mention of two additional cardinal points. First, it is possible for a class of operant behavior to be strengthened considerably as a consequence of a *single* reinforcement. In general, we would expect such strengthening to take place if (1) the interval between operant and reinforcer was very short, (2) the reinforcer was very powerful (e.g., food after prolonged fasting, or a strong electric shock delivered to the feet), (3) the operant was a simple one, and (4) it had already been fairly well strengthened in a similar situation.

Second, it is the *number of times that a response has been reinforced* that strengthens the operant interaction, not the number of responses that have occurred. Investigations have shown repeatedly that the mere repetition of a response is not automatically strengthening. Hence, practice does *not* make perfect unless (1) each response leads directly or indirectly (that is, through a chain of events) to a natural or conditioned reinforcer, and (2) the setting event is appropriate, that is, does not unduly weaken the reinforcing property of the stimulus or strengthen responses that are in competition with the operant, such as fatigue-generated responses. These findings deserve careful consideration because of their far-reaching implications, both practical and theoretical.

REFERENCES

SKINNER, B.F., *Cumulative Record* (3rd ed.). Englewood Cliffs, N.J.: Prentice-Hall, 1972.

7

Maintenance of Operant
Interactions Through
Schedules of Reinforcement

In Chapters 5 and 6 we focused on the conditions that *establish* stimulus and response functions in an operant interaction, that is, the conditions under which they are acquired or learned. Now we consider the conditions which *maintain* stimulus and response operant functions. In the traditional literature, this aspect of psychological behavior is referred to as retention, memory, or remembering.

When we come to consider the behavior of the organism in all the complexity of its everyday life, we need to be constantly alert to the prevailing reinforcements which maintain its behavior. We may, indeed, have little interest in how that behavior was first acquired. Our concern is only with its present probability of occurrence, which can be understood only through an examination of current contingencies of reinforcement (Skinner, 1953, p. 98).

The current contingencies of reinforcement to which Skinner refers have been studied intensively in the experimental laboratory (e.g., Ferster & Skinner, 1957) and are called *schedules of reinforcements.* We shall describe only two kinds of schedules—continuous and intermittent, the behavior patterns they generate (e.g., slow and steady, fast and steady, fast and erratic), and the critical uses of these schedules in applied behavior analysis, particularly in teaching and training.

CONTINUOUS REINFORCEMENT

When operant behavior is reinforced every time it occurs, the relationship is known as a schedule of *continuous reinforcement.* Such a schedule has two characteristics: (1) It strengthens the preceding class of operant behavior rapidly and produces a regular pattern of responding, and (2)

If a response strengthened by continuous reinforcement is extinguished, its strength returns to its operant level relatively quickly, but during the extinction process the response reoccurs irregularly in considerable strength. Initial nonreinforcement of a response that has been reinforced previously may result in momentarily increasing the response rate and may generate other behavior, e.g., shouting at the person or hitting the object that seems "responsible" for the cessation of reinforcement. Continual nonreinforcement eventually will lead to responding at the operant level of that class of responses.

A continuous schedule of reinforcement is the basic schedule for the first systematic strengthening of a response in an individual's reinforcement history (demand feeding); it is the schedule inherent in the action of most natural reinforcers (Ferster, 1967). (Moving away from a hot fire invariably reduces or removes a negative reinforcer.) The initial phase of teaching is usually done by continuous reinforcement to promote efficiency of learning. When introducing a child to the first reading lesson, an experienced teacher, whether aware of it or not, reinforces each correct response with praise, a star, or some other effective reinforcer. But otherwise, people rarely reinforce other people by continuous reinforcement, except when deliberately trying to teach a new response to someone else (particularly a child). Because parents, teachers, etc. are often involved in other activities while interacting with a child, they give reinforcers in a rather haphazard way for what they consider to be correct or desirable responses.

Some continuous reinforcement schedules have a rate-of-response contingency. In one simple example of this schedule, the reinforcer is given only if a *long* interval has elapsed since the last response. This schedule, referred to as *differential reinforcement of low rate,* is used mainly to slow down the rate of responding. For example, it is effective in helping a babbling child to talk or read at a slower pace (thereby improving the ability to communicate). In another simple type, the reinforcer is given only if there has been a *short* interval since the last response. This schedule, called *differential reinforcement of high rate,* increases the response rate and may be used to help a hesitant child talk or read *faster,* and in that way improve ability in verbal-social interactions.

INTERMITTENT REINFORCEMENT

We noted above that in everyday life a class of response is not generally reinforced each time it occurs. Most often, we reinforce it on some sort of an intermittent basis. Studies of the effects of various kinds of *inter-*

mittent reinforcement have revealed some surprising findings. These studies help us understand children's development through an analysis of their particular reinforcement histories.

Ratio Schedules of Reinforcement

One way in which a response class may be reinforced intermittently is by making the reinforcer contingent upon the *number of responses;* that is, a response class is reinforced every Nth time it occurs. A manufacturer might pay an employee 10¢ for every twenty units produced (this is known as "piecework"); a slot machine might pay off with a jackpot (of perhaps $10) for approximately every 100 quarters put in it. Both of these practices reinforce the individual on the basis of how many responses (sometimes in the form of products) were made, and are called *ratio schedules.* That is, there will be a ratio of one reinforcer to N responses. The effect of a ratio schedule, as might be guessed from these examples, is to generate a great many rapid responses for a rather small amount of reinforcement. The manufacturer who pays employees 10 cents for every twenty units produced is interested in getting many responses (work) from the employees in a short period of time. That use of a ratio schedule is shrewd, because this is precisely the effect of ratio schedules. In particular, the higher the ratio, the faster the rate of response it produces (one reinforcer per 20 responses is a "higher" ratio than one reinforcer per 10 responses).

The two examples given above differ in one important respect. Giving 10 cents for every 20 pieces of work completed is a perfectly predictable reinforcement situation, in that the reinforcer comes at fixed points. This is an example of a *fixed ratio schedule.* On the other hand, when a slot machine gives back money, it does not do it for a predictable response. Instead, it reinforces the player, on the average, for every 100 quarters put into it. In practice, it might reinforce (pay off) for the 97th quarter, then the 153rd, then the 178th, then the 296th, then the 472nd, then the 541st, then the 704th, etc. The average ratio of such a series might be one reinforcer per 100 responses, but the number of unreinforced responses between reinforcements is variable. Therefore it is called a *variable ratio schedule.* Its effect is to generate a high rate of responding, as do fixed ratio schedules. But if the reinforcers finally stop altogether, then response after variable ratio reinforcement proves more durable than response after fixed ratio reinforcement, and much more durable than response after continuous reinforcement. These facts are particularly relevant to child development, because there are many situations in which children will be reinforced on a ratio basis. We will be able to understand the children's behavior patterns in those situations better if we keep in mind the rate of response and its durability after the reinforcers stop. A boy may be on a fixed ratio schedule of reinforcement in school. He may be assigned 50 arithmetic problems and told that when he is finished he may do something else, presumably something reinforcing, such as selecting his favorite jigsaw puzzle and putting it together. We expect a fast rate of response in doing the problems. A girl at home may be told that she must finish her reading homework assignment before she can go out to play. Again, we expect a fast rate, because she is on a fixed ratio schedule—so many pages read and questions answered to one reinforcer. (Note that "pages read" and "material comprehended" are two different behaviors.) A boy may discover that when his mother is watching her favorite TV program, he has to ask her many times for something he wants before he can crack through her shell of preoccupation. This is a variable ratio; his mother will answer more quickly some times than other times. If this is a frequent occurrence, we expect that repetitive requests at a rapid rate will become a strong response characteristic of that boy, and that if he is switched to a different reinforcement schedule, or is no longer reinforced, the response characteristic will be slow to extinguish.

Variable ratio schedules of reinforcement that systematically *increase* and *decrease* the ratio of reinforcers play an important role in child development, in both its informal and formal teaching aspects. Teaching manners in the family setting is an example of the first type; teaching academic subjects either in the home or the school is an example of the second type. An *increasing ratio schedule* systematically provides less reinforcement without decreasing performance rate. For example, reinforcers are provided after every five correct responses for a while, then after every 10 for a while, and then after every 15, etc., for as long as they adequately maintain the behavior. The rate of successive changes in response requirement (from five to 10 to 15 in the above example) is a function of the child's performance. Changes in the number of responses required for a reinforcer are made as long as the rate of responding remains at the desired level. If performance decreases or becomes erratic, the thinning procedure is terminated for a while, and if that increases performance to the desired rate, the ratio is decreased again. An increasing ratio schedule is one of the most effective techniques for helping a child to work on larger and larger segments of a task and is often used to increase attention span and independent work or play. On the other hand, a *decreasing ratio schedule* systematically provides more reinforcers, that is, a richer distribution of reinforcers for the acquisition or maintenance of a response. Thus, a ratio schedule of one reinforcer for every 15 responses may be changed to one reinforcer for every 10 responses, and then one for every five. A decreasing ratio schedule is generally put into effect temporarily, when a child's performance decreases or becomes erratic. Such a schedule is often recommended to parents who otherwise would reinforce their child too sparsely.

Interval Schedules of Reinforcement

Another way in which operant responses may be reinforced intermittently is on the basis of *time passing* rather than on number of responses. In this case, the response is reinforced the first time it occurs after N minutes (the units could be hours, days, weeks, or months) have passed since the last time it was reinforced. This kind of schedule is called an *interval schedule,* to denote its reliance on a time interval between any two reinforcers. An employer pays employees every Friday afternoon. A professor reinforces students' studying by giving them a quiz every Monday. A mother decides that her boy can have the cookie he has asked for because it has been "long enough" since the last one. In all of these examples, it is not response output that determines the next reinforcement occasion, but simply the passage of time, and time cannot be hurried by responding. The employees have worked for a week; the students have studied for the weekly quiz; the child has waited for an approved interval; etc. In no case is the reinforcer given "free;" it is given as a consequence of a response— the first response occurring after a given time has passed since the last reinforcer.

An interval schedule in which the time between reinforced responses is constant is called a *fixed interval schedule;* one that is not constant, a *variable interval schedule.* In the examples above, the payment of wages every Friday afternoon and the quizzing of students every Monday are fixed interval schedules; the mother giving her child a cookie because "it has been long enough since the last one" is a variable interval schedule.

Probably the most interesting characteristic of the fixed interval schedule of reinforcement is that after its effects have stabilized, it produces a period of practically no responding followed by an acceleration of responding until the occurrence of the next reinforcer. In other words, a slow production period is followed by a fast production period. (Can this empirical finding be related to the fact that in most factories where employees are paid on a weekly basis absenteeism is greatest at the beginning of the week?)

The variable interval schedule, on the other hand, produces extremely durable interactions that continue at a slow, even rate long after the reinforcers have ceased. This suggests that behaviors strengthened through reinforcement on variable interval schedules may survive for long periods without reinforcers, or will continue even when reinforcers are exceedingly irregular and infrequent. A child may engage in a certain behavior only a few times a day, which only rarely seems to be reinforced in any way that an observer can detect, yet it retains its strength. The explanation often lies primarily in the variable interval schedule on which that behavior is now reinforced or has been reinforced in the past.

The nagging behavior of a child (begging, whining, sleeve tugging, and the like) is a response that is sometimes reinforced on a variable ratio schedule (when the child has nagged enough times, the parent gives in), but more often is reinforced on a variable interval basis (when the parent thinks it has been long enough since the last reinforcer, or when the child acts this way in public, or when the parent is tired, a reinforcer will be given). The interval often may be a long one, particularly when parents think they can discourage nagging by not complying. In principle, this practice is perfect; provided that nagging is never reinforced, it will extinguish. But typical parents do not quite manage *never* to reinforce nagging; on rare occasions, in moments of some weakness, such as being irritable, embarrassed before company, etc., they succumb. These occasional reinforcements generate a history of variable interval reinforcement of nagging, which contributes greatly to its strength and durability. Consequently, even if the parents should manage never again to reinforce nagging, it will be a long time and many responses until it finally extinguishes. Even *one* reinforcement during this extinction regime may re-establish the response in considerable strength.

This example shows how a class of operant behavior may be impervious to change for a long period, even with a minimum of reinforcement, because of its past schedule of reinforcement. In talking about children's personalities, one often hears traits described that are firm and persistent in their behavior but seem to have no obvious source of reinforcement in their current environments. Nagging, temper tantrums, and whining are typical examples. The explanation for many such generally undesirable personality characteristics is almost always a past history of reinforcement on a variable interval basis.

Two kinds of interval schedules deserve special attention: *increasing interval and decreasing interval.* Increasing interval schedules in which the intervals between reinforcement become greater are considered "weaning" schedules because they help a child to work independently for increasingly longer periods. On the other hand, decreasing interval schedules that provide a child with additional support are effective for many kinds of remediation.

Both ratio and interval reinforcement schedules sustain a great deal of behavior with a small number of reinforcers. Ratio schedules may generate a large number of responses at rapid rates for each reinforcer; interval schedules may result in moderate but stable rates of responding over long time intervals between reinforcers. It is important to emphasize, however, that these extremely stretched-out schedules cannot be used successfully at the beginning of learning; they must be developed gradually from schedules in which responses, at least at first, are reinforced nearly every time they occur (continuous reinforcement). Once a response has been strengthened by continuous or nearly continuous reinforcement, the schedule may shift through a series of increasing ratios or increasing intervals to the point where an extremely powerful or durable response is attained and maintained by a minimal number of reinforcers. This concept of developing strong, stable behavior through the gradually shifting, thinning-out schedules of reinforcement is perhaps one of the most serviceable conceptual tools available for analyzing a child's psychological development.

Still another important interval schedule is one with *aversive* characteristics. In this kind of interaction, the response avoids a negative reinforcer. For example, a child may notice an ominous frown on her mother's face and quickly volunteer to wash the dishes. Perhaps this will erase the frown, which to the child is a discriminative stimulus for impending negative reinforcement like a scolding or a restriction of privileges. But the effect of this removal of a negative reinforcer may be temporary. In time, it may appear that some other "helpful" response is necessary to delay another imminent blow-up of the parent. Studies have been made in the laboratory of aversive schedules that produce a negative reinforcer at fixed time intervals (e.g., every 30 seconds), unless a certain response is made. When the effect of the response is to put off the impending negative reinforcer for another period (say another 30 seconds), this contingency between the response and the delay of the next negative reinforcer is sufficient to gradually strengthen the response. In fact, the response often increases to the point where it successfully avoids virtually all of the scheduled negative reinforcers. In this case, we see a response made at a steady rate which is apparently very durable but we do not see any reinforcement contingency supporting the response. The reason for this apparent independence of the response from a reinforcement contingency is, of course, that the response of perfectly avoiding the negative reinforcer is maintained by discriminative stimuli. The response may be tied closely to a particular discriminative stimulus like a frown, or may be controlled only by the less obvious stimuli provided by the passage of time. For example, a father who is frequently angry (but in an unpredictable way) may be placated by his children during the day, just because it has been "a while" since his last outburst. That "while" is a stimulus that is discriminative for the next one coming up soon. The placating behavior then may be viewed as one that is maintained because it avoids negative reinforcers, that is, it is reinforced on a schedule with an aversive contingency.

The aversive schedule is often an essential characteristic of some social situations because it sets up extremely strong and lasting responses that persist without obvious reinforcement: they are successful responses exactly because they keep the reinforcement from becoming obvious. An example is "You're welcome." Saying it would not get us much, but omitting it would. Thus, this schedule, like the other schedules discussed, is useful in analyzing many childhood interactions, especially those referred to as manners.

SUMMARY

We have presented only a small sample of the ways in which simple schedules of reinforcement maintain learned behavior with certain characteristics and strengthen acquired reinforcers. Knowing the schedules in effect aids in understanding what has happened and is happening in many situations with a child. From the practical point of view, knowing the behavioral characteristics that are associated with schedules of reinforcement is helpful to the parent, teacher, and therapist in remedying problem behaviors. However, one must remember that in a child's everyday interactions, these simple schedules are mixed and combined in very complex ways, so that the relationships described here may rarely be seen in isolation.

REFERENCES

FERSTER, C.B., Arbitrary and natural reinforcement. *Psychological Record,* 1967, *17,* 341-47.

FERSTER, C.B. AND SKINNER, B.F., *Schedules of Reinforcement.* Englewood Cliffs, N.J.: Prentice-Hall, 1957.

SKINNER, B.F., *Science and Human Behavior.* New York: Macmillan, 1953.

8

Discrimination
and Generalization

"In the ever changing environment, the generalization of stimuli gives stability and consistency to our behavior . . . in contrast with generalization, the process of discrimination gives our behavior its specificity, variety, and flexibility." (Keller & Schoenfeld, 1950, 116-117.)

DISCRIMINATION

The concept of discrimination might best be introduced with some examples. A preadolescent boy observes the frown on his father's face and hears his irritated voice commenting on the lateness of dinner; he decides that he had better not ask for an advance on his allowance. The frown and the voice are stimuli marking an occasion on which a request for more allowance probably will fail to be reinforced; his father will refuse. Later, observing his father sitting in his comfortable chair, feet up, and puffing away on his pipe, the boy makes the request, which, perhaps after a reasonable discussion, is reinforced with a promise of more money.

A red traffic light for a pedestrian is a stimulus marking an occasion when crossing the street may be negatively reinforced, either by being knocked down by a car or being cited by a policeman. A green light, however, marks an occasion when crossing the street will avoid these negative reinforcers, and will get one further on the way toward other reinforcers, such as keeping an appointment with a friend.

The buzzing of an alarm clock is a stimulus signaling the time to get up. If we turn it off and go back to sleep, we suffer the punishment of being late to class or to work.

Friday is the name of a day of the week, and for many people it is a time when going to work will be reinforced with the weekly paycheck, and a coming time (Saturday) that will not contain the negative reinforcers that force them daily to their jobs. Friday night often signals a time when the alarm clock need not be set.

In these examples, we have seen many preceding stimuli that influence our behaviors, not because they elicit respondent behaviors as described in Chapter 4, but because they promise various reinforcements. Any such stimulus is said to have a *discriminative* functional property, and is defined as one that marks, cues, or signals a probable time or place of reinforcers, positive or negative, being presented or removed.

You will recall our insistence earlier that the strength of operant behavior is related to its stimulus consequences, whereas the strength of respondent behavior is related to its stimulus antecedents. Now we may seem to be blurring this clear distinction by saying that operant behavior is controlled by preceding *as well as* by consequent stimulation. The distinction, nevertheless, still holds, because its crucial feature remains unchanged: a preceding discriminative stimulus controls an operant *only* because it marks a time or place when that operant probably will have some kind of reinforcing consequence. A discriminative stimulus does not have an elicitation function. Elicitation is a property of stimuli *only* in respondent interactions. The green traffic light does not set us going across the street in the same way that a bright light flashed in our eyes constricts our pupils. The pupillary response is physically controlled by the bright light, quite independently of its consequences; crossing the street (an operant) is controlled by the green light as a result of having learned the special consequences of crossing the street at that time, as opposed to other (red light) times, and because of our history of reinforcement and extinction in relation to green, amber, and red traffic lights. The important characteristic of operant behavior is its sensitivity to stimulus consequences; however, preceding stimuli may control operant behavior as cues to the nature of contingent stimulation.

Whenever we see an individual consistently displaying a certain class of operant responses in close conjunction with a class of stimuli that marks a probable reinforcement occasion, we refer to that response as a *discriminated operant response,* that is, one controlled by a stimulus with discriminative function in the context of an appropriate setting event. A person who typically responds in relation to discriminative stimuli is said to be discriminating, and the procedure of bringing operant behavior under such control is called discrimination. We may diagram the *general* case of discriminative operant interaction as follows:

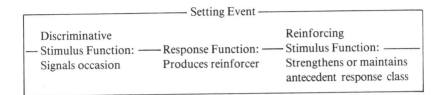

The diagram is read as follows: a stimulus with the function of a positive reinforcer strengthens the preceding class of behavior, but only in the presence of a stimulus with a discriminative function and in the context of a setting event. Notice that this diagram is similar to the diagram of a simple operant on page 54. The only difference is that this one includes a *preceding* stimulus. In analyzing a discriminative operant interaction we take into account four interdependent conditions: the setting event, the antecedent stimulus with a discriminative function, the response with an effecting function, and the consequent stimulus with a reinforcing function. A discriminative operant interaction may be referred to as the *four-term contingency.*

The process of operant discrimination has crucial significance for the analysis of developmental psychology. Consider that the infant is born, genetically ready to be reinforced by a number of stimuli (milk, temperature, sleep, oxygen, open diaper pins, ammonia, etc.) but thoroughly unacquainted with the stimuli that signal the occasions on which these reinforcers will be present. A great part of psychological development is, therefore, simply the process of learning the discriminative stimuli that signal important reinforcers. Mothers are discriminative stimuli for many reinforcers: they bring milk, adjust the temperature with sweaters and blankets, rock babies to sleep, rescue them from open pins, change their wet, irritating diapers, and so forth. Later in life, children may learn that their mothers' approval, a particular stimulus they can provide, is a discriminative stimulus for other important reinforcers: cookies, permission to play outside or to stay overnight at a friend's house, the purchase of a bicycle, and the like. Still later, they may learn that possession of a car is an important discriminative stimulus for the behaviors of others who are reinforcing to them—it is a stimulus that brings them the respect and approval of their teenage peers, the ability to move fast and far for entertainment, and an entry to lover's lane. In short, we can say a great deal about child development simply by attending to the discriminations children make as they grow, because these discriminative stimuli will control their behavior. As a matter of fact, this area of study is referred to as *stimulus control.*

Modeling or Imitation

In the instances and examples given above, the form of the discriminative stimulus, such as the buzzing of an alarm clock, and the form of the operant behavior, such as reaching for the clock and pressing the alarm lever are not similar. However, there are discriminative operant situations in which the form of the discriminative stimulus and the form of the operant behavior are similar. We refer to these interactions as modeling or imitation. The similarity may be the *structure* of the discriminative stimulus and operant behavior. Thus a discriminative stimulus may be a mother's clapping her hands and the setting event of "Do this," and the operant response may be her baby's clapping hands (and sometimes adding, "Do this"). On the other hand, the similarity may be the *products* of behavior. A discriminative stimulus of this sort may be demonstrating the drawing of a circle together with the instruction "Make one like this," and the operant response, a child drawing a circle on paper. In both structure and product imitation, the model's behavior is reinforced by the child's imitative operant response which in turn is reinforced by the model saying something like "Good for you." It should be clear that *modeling or imitation is analyzed here as discriminative operant interaction* and not as a separate and distinct learning process nor as an interaction involving cognitive factors and processes (Bandura, 1977).

Does this analysis of imitation suggest how you might interpret negativistic behavior in children?

Abstract or Conceptualizing Interactions

Operant behavior can not only come under the control of any antecedent stimuli, it can come under the control of one or more *aspects* of antecedent stimuli such as color, form, texture, and size. When a child is responding to an aspect or aspects of antecedent stimuli, he is said to be engaging in an *abstract or conceptualizing interaction.* We can give this contrast: in a simple discriminative operant interaction a child responds to differences *between* stimulus classes (hardware versus clothing) whereas in conceptualizing interaction he responds to a common aspect or aspects of stimuli *within* stimulus classes (grouping hardware items on the basis of material or use, and grouping clothing on the basis of fabric or function).

Since the isolated properties of antecedent stimulus do not occur under natural conditions, individuals in a child's environment must arrange conditions for a child to respond to aspects of things and thereby learn concepts. A mother who in the normal course of family living names things ("That's a flower"), points out the critical features of similar objects ("A tricycle has three wheels"), draws out conceptual behavior ("What do you call that?"), encourages and confirms an appropriate response ("Yes, that's a car"), and gently corrects misconceptions ("That's not a pony; it's a big dog") provides a positive, stimulating home situation which, among other things, is conducive to conceptual learning. It should be apparent from what has been said thus far that mere exposure to a variety of interesting objects and events—conditions which correlate very high with the socioeconomic status of the family— does nothing to guarantee that a child will acquire the essential concepts of his society. A rich environment must include people *who are able and willing* to help a child respond differentially to the properties of objects and events in his everyday encounters.

GENERALIZATION

Typically, we find that when children learn that a certain discriminative stimulus marks a reinforcement occasion, they will behave under the control of that discriminative stimulus and also of other stimuli similar to it. For example, a young girl may be powerfully reinforced by candy. Suppose that her father often brings home a little bag of candy, and, on arriving, calls out "Candy!" The girl will soon learn to approach her father very quickly when she hears him call "Candy " because this distinctive social stimulus sets an occasion when the behavior of her approaching father will be positively reinforced. Prior to this experience, the spoken word "Candy" was undoubtedly a neutral stimulus for this toddler, controlling none of her behaviors in a functional way. Now, as a consequence of its discriminative status for positive reinforcement following an approach response, we find it a powerful stimulus in controlling some of her behavior. Furthermore, we will probably find that other sounds that resemble the word "candy" will also set the occasion for a quick approach to her father. As an example, if her father calls upstairs to her mother, "Can you please hurry a bit so we'll be on time?", the loud "Can . . ." may be sufficiently like the "Candy!" that has been the discriminative stimulus to set the occasion for a quick charge by the toddler toward her father. For a time, many loud words with an initial "ka" sound may serve as generalized discriminative stimuli.

Whenever some particular stimulus, through association with reinforcement, takes on discriminative functions, other stimuli (even though not associated directly with the reinforcement) will also demonstrate discriminative functions, to the extent that they are similar to the original discriminative stimulus. This characteristic of our reaction to the environment is called *stimulus generalization.*

Generalization may be thought of as a failure to discriminate. That is, one discriminative stimulus has signaled reinforcement occasions; other stimuli have not. However, because some of these other stimuli are like this first discriminative stimulus in some respect, they are responded to as if they, too, signal an occasion for the same reinforcement. Thus, the child is not discriminating accurately. We would expect that with repeated experiences in which the original discriminative stimulus is associated with reinforcement, and other merely similar stimuli are responded to but are not followed by reinforcement, discrimination would improve. Hence, the similar but unreinforced stimuli would lose their function to evoke behavior, while the original and reinforced discriminative stimulus would retain its function. Typically, this is true.

The discrimination process is described technically in terms of the strengthening of the response through reinforcement and the weakening of the response through extinction (non-reinforcement, discussed on pages 54-59). Reinforcing a response in the presence of particular stimuli, as we have just said, makes it more likely that the response will occur in similar stimulus situations. However, repeated responding in other situations without reinforcing consequences leads to the extinction of the response—in these other stimulus situations. Meanwhile, repeated reinforced responding in the original stimulus situation increases and maintains the strength of the response—in the original stimulus situation. While it is obvious that strengthening and weakening procedures can affect a response simultaneously in specific stimulus situations, such procedures do not necessarily affect the strength of the response in general. We see, then, that in order to give an operant class a high probability of occurrence in a specific (discriminative) stimulus situation and a low probability of occurrence in all other stimulus situations, we must strengthen the operant behavior in the discriminative stimulus situation and extinguish it in all other situations.[1] Note that we have described discrimination as a combination of reinforcement in one stimulus situation, extinction in another. This is the common procedure. However, a more general treatment of discrimination should point out that all that is required is reinforcement of a response in one situation, and *any different* treatment of the response in another. Thus, the response might be reinforced in one situation, and it might be extinguished, or punished, or even reinforced in another situation, but not as effectively as in the first situation. A discrimination should form in any case. Could you not discriminate between two identical jobs, one of which pays $5 an hour and the other $4 an hour?

To the extent that behavior has been strengthened in one situation and weakened in another, an operant class will become finely tuned to the specific antecedent stimulus desired. This is one meaning of "skill." Another meaning of skill involves selecting one specific response class to reinforce while extinguishing all other variations of the response, even though they are similar to the desired response. *Just as stimuli generalize, so do responses.* Strengthening one response directly results in an indirect strengthening of other responses, insofar as they are like the original response. This, it will be recalled, is referred to as *response induction,* which is the same as response generalization. However, any response that grows in strength because it is like a reinforced response can be extinguished separately, leaving the reinforced response in a precise form. This procedure, shaping (see pages 59-64), is *response differentiation,* a term which is parallel to stimulus discrimination.

Learning to hit a baseball involves both stimulus discrimination and response differentiation. When a girl swings at a baseball pitched within her reach, the chain of responses involved is reinforced and strengthened by occasional hits. When she swings at a ball thrown outside her reach, the motor sequence constituting the act of swinging is extinguished by a high frequency of misses. (More often it is punished by teammates and spectators.) Thus her batting becomes more accurate; in other words, she swings more frequently at pitches that are likely to be hit. Further refinement usually follows. A particular pitch within hitting range (like one that comes over the plate and is about waist-high) may come to evoke a special swing that connects with the ball. This precise swing is reinforced,

---

[1]In the study of Jones described on page 39, the "emotional" stimulus (a rabbit that elicited crying) was extinguished more quickly by simultaneously making it discriminative for candy reinforcers.

while others that are somewhat like it (but different in that they do not hit the ball) are extinguished or punished. In this way, batting becomes ever more precise and a given pitch (discriminative stimulus) is soon responded to with that swing (differentiated response) most likely to hit the ball.

We said that a large part of child development means learning the discriminative stimuli that signal important reinforcement occasions. Another way of saying the same thing, but approaching it from the opposite direction, is that a large part of child development is learning how far to generalize, in some situations called, "testing the limits."

Indeed, in the application of a behavioral analysis to the practical problems of educating children and correcting their behavior problems, the procedure for adequate generalization is often the most ensuring critical part of good teaching or good therapy. How to change a behavior is often quite clear; how to make sure that the behavior changes similarly in all relevant settings, and/or that related behaviors change in the same way, as well, is the problem. Thus, speech therapists often complain that they can change a child's misarticulation of certain language sounds in their clinic, but that the child continues to misarticulate everywhere else; teachers complain that they can establish good grammar in their classroom, but that the same grammatical constructions will be used improperly outside of that room; parents complain that their child's good behavior, so obvious at school, does not seem to extend to their home. In each instance, it is too narrow a generalization that is at issue, and broader generalization would be a solution to the problem.

Stokes and Baer (1976) have surveyed the techniques currently in use in applied behavioral work to solve such problems. Consider some paraphrased selections from their catalog of methods:

1. Do not depend on generalization at all; instead, make the behavior changes directly in every setting or case that requires it. For example, if a child's stuttering can be eliminated by a certain type of electronically managed auditory feedback, and if treatment in a clinic setting has not eliminated stuttering in home and classrooms settings, then bring the necessary electronic apparatus to the home and the classroom and apply the same treatment there that was applied in the clinic.

2. Be sure to teach enough examples of the new behavior, or teach it in enough examples of the settings in which it should occur. For example, when teaching a child how to do long division, do not teach the algorithm of steps for only one example; instead, teach it again and again, using different numbers, and numbers of different lengths, in each successive

example. Typically, behavior that does not generalize after being taught once (often to the surprise of the teacher, who has long since learned the general lesson and perhaps because of that thinks that all students need only one example) will generalize very well after as few as two to five diverse examples. (It is probably good sense to make the examples as different as possible, but at the same time to be sure that the most difficult ones are encountered last.) One of the practical translations of this general principle is to use two teachers when establishing a difficult behavior change with children, especially children with severe behavior problems or severe developmental deficits. Often it is found that a behavior change accomplished by one teacher will be evident only in the presence of that teacher, yet the same behavior change, taught by two teachers, may well generalize to all possible other persons.

3. Be sure that there are some important, salient stimuli present in the teaching situation that will also be present in the other settings to which the new behavior should generalize. An increasingly used tactic in this regard is the use of peer-tutors. Thus, a child with an articulation problem may be taught in a clinic setting, not directly by a speech therapist, but by a peer—a classmate, perhaps, or a friend from the home neighborhood, or a sibling—who is taught how to do that aspect of speech therapy by the speech therapist. So the therapist coaches the peer, who prompts the classmate, who responds, and the therapist prompts the peer to reinforce, or correct, or whatever is needed. Although this kind of teaching may proceed a little more slowly than if the speech therapist did it directly, it may generalize much more quickly and thoroughly than would be the case otherwise. In short, wherever a child goes and encounters the peer, *or others like the peer,* the proper articulation may well appear. The peer, of course, is a discriminative stimulus for that proper articulation, and a discriminative stimulus that is likely to be present in the correct settings, settings in which the therapist can hardly be present.

4. Try to avoid making it clear where reinforcement for desirable behavior is possible and where it is not. A useful, although somewhat limited, technique to aid in this attempt is delayed reinforcement. Suppose, for example, that we mean to correct a child's posture in school, and can make TV tapes of the child in various classrooms during the school day. We might (as one study did) show the tapes to the child at the end of the day and give as much reinforcement as there was good posture to be seen in the tapes. By not making it clear whether the tapes were from one classroom or another, we might be able to prevent any discrimination of the form, say, that posture is important in spelling class but not in arith-

metic class. However, remember that delayed reinforcement can sometimes be too weak to accomplish anything, let alone a generalized behavior change.

5. Sometimes we can use one response to mediate the generalization of
another. In the section on Self-Management in Chapter 11, there is a discussion of this possibility, but we will mention here a technique used by
Rogers-Warren and Baer (1976) to illustrate the same process. Their subjects were preschool children. The goal of the study was to develop better
skills of sharing and praising art work. Those behaviors might have been
reinforced directly as they occurred, but this would have required extensive
and careful observation of the children's behavior by the teacher, and also
would have interrupted the sometimes complex behaviors making up
sharing and praising. Perhaps such behaviors develop better without
interruption, even for reinforcement. Consequently, the investigators
had observers carefully observe the children during their art work. Afterwards, the teacher, knowing who had praised and shared from those
observations relayed to her, asked the children, "Who shared today?" or,
later, "Who praised today?" (in language suitable for the children's
developmental abilities). Those who truthfully reported doing so received
reinforcers. This was sufficient to increase the children's rates of sharing
and praising (depending on which kinds of verbal reports were being reinforced at the time). It is important to remember that it was not the
sharing and praising behaviors that were reinforced, but only the subsequent reports by the children that they had already shared or praised.
Apparently, attaching reinforcement to true reports of sharing and praising
was sufficient to induce the children to actually share and praise the next
day, so that at the end of that day's activities they could truthfully report
that they had done so, and be reinforced. We can say that the verbal behavior that gained the reinforcers also mediated the praising and sharing
behavior that it was about. In general, this can be a vital function of
language behavior; its nature makes it ideal for mediating other behavioral
changes at other times, for our language is always with us, wherever we
go. Indeed, at its best, language is a versatile repertory that can describe
virtually any facet of our behavior and our environments. Note, however,
that language need not mediate; to say that it can is not to guarantee that
it will. The conditions necessary to guarantee that language will mediate the
behavior specified in its content are not yet thoroughly clear, but in the
Rogers-Warren and Baer study, it was important to reinforce only *true*
reports of sharing or praising. Otherwise, children might report falsely
that they had shared or praised, and so earn the offered reinforcers with-

out changing their actual sharing and praising behaviors. In that case, their language definitely would not be mediating their sharing and praising; it would simply be exploiting the person giving the reinforcers.

REFERENCES

BANDURA, A., *Social Learning Theory.* Englewood Cliffs, N.J.: Prentice-Hall, 1977.

KELLER, F.S. AND SCHOENFELD, W.N., *Principles of Psychology.* New York: Appleton-Century-Crofts, Inc., 1950.

ROGER-WARREN, A. AND BAER, D.M., Correspondence between saying and doing: Teaching children to share and praise. *Journal of Applied Behavior Analysis,* 1976, *9,* 335-54.

STOKES, T.F. & BAER, D.M., Preschool peers as mutual generalization-facilitation agents. *Behavior Therapy,* 1976, *7,* 549-556.

9

Acquired Reinforcers
and Multiple Stimulus
and Response Functions

Consider again the example in Chapter 8 of the boy who recognized that his father's frown was a discriminative stimulus indicating the time when a request for an increase in allowance would not be likely to get good results, that is, be positively reinforced. We predicted that he would wait for the occurrence of a different set of discriminative stimuli (e.g., the father sitting with his feet up, smiling, reading the comics, and smoking his pipe) that would indicate a more favorable reinforcement possibility. Another prediction would also be reasonable: if he could discover a better way than just waiting to replace his father's frown with a smile, he would certainly try it. If he was successful in producing the right discriminative stimulus from his father, he would ask for the increase. In technical terms, if a response removes a discriminative stimulus indicating the probability of extinction or punishment (the frown), it is strengthened; if a response results in a discriminative stimulus signaling the probability of positive reinforcement (a smile, chuckle, etc.), that response is also strengthened. This fishing for ways of producing desirable discriminative stimuli may be observed often in everyday life. They are called by many names, such as persuasion, flattery, coercion, logical argument, and distraction. Note that the response contingencies in the above statement are precisely the test used to establish stimuli as reinforcers: if a response that produces a stimulus is strengthened thereby, that stimulus is a positive reinforcer; if a response that removes or avoids a stimulus is strengthened thereby, that stimulus is a negative reinforcer (see pages 44-54). Can a stimulus have both discriminative and reinforcing properties? According to the definitions given, the answer is yes. Later in this chapter, we shall see that a stimulus can have more than two functions.

ACQUIRED REINFORCER FUNCTIONS

Our discussion, coupled with readily observable facts of behavior, lead to this formulation: when a stimulus acquires a discriminative function, it also acquires a reinforcing function. In particular, a discriminative stimulus that signals the probability of positive reinforcement, or the removal of negative reinforcers, functions as a *positive* reinforcer. A discriminative stimulus that indicates the probability of encountering negative reinforcers, the removal of positive reinforcers, or extinction, functions as a negative reinforcer. Reinforcers, positive or negative, that have achieved their reinforcing property through prior (or current) service as discriminative stimuli are called *acquired reinforcers* to denote that they have resulted from a conditioning or learning process. (Acquired reinforcers are often called secondary, conditioned, or learned reinforcers. All four terms are used synonymously here.) The equation of a discriminative stimulus with an acquired reinforcer means that the same stimulus in different situations may (1) reinforce any preceding operants, and (2) provide a cue for the occurrence or non-occurrence of the particular operants whose reinforcing consequences it signalled in the past.

Using the example of a child eating custard (Chapter 5), we can diagram a sequence with a dual function stimulus:

Mild Food Deprivation: Setting Event			
Custard in -Bowl: ——— Discriminative S for R 1	Response 1 (R 1): ——— Looking and Bringing to Mouth	Custard in Mouth: ——— Reinforcing S for R 1 and Discriminative S for R 2	Response 2 (R 2): ——— Looking and Bringing to Mouth

We can read the diagram this way: under the setting condition of mild food deprivation, the response of bringing a spoonful of custard to the mouth is dependent on whether there is custard in the bowl. Custard in the bowl is a discriminative stimulus for scooping some of it out with a spoon and bringing to the mouth (R1). A spoonful of custard in the mouth is a reinforcing stimulus for the preceding skillful behavior (R1) and the remaining custard in the bowl is a discriminative stimulus for scooping some more custard and bringing it to the mouth (R2).

We said previously that much of human development could be understood by investigating the ways in which a child learns about the world, that is, the discriminative stimuli that indicate a high probability of reinforcements. It should be clear now that an important part of development consists of the child's learning what responses produce certain discriminative stimuli and remove or avoid other discriminative stimuli. Indeed, many of the reinforcers linked with our social behavior are acquired reinforcers, as, for example, approval and disapproval, social status, prestige, attention, and affection. Much of child psychology consists of analyzing the child's personal history to show where and how such stimuli first served as discriminative stimuli for other, earlier reinforcers, such as milk. An analysis along these lines goes a long way toward describing and explaining what is commonly called the child's "personality." (A detailed account of such events is given in Bijou & Baer, 1965, Pp. 65-70.)

A second procedural variation for developing an acquired reinforcer is to pair a neutral stimulus with a known reinforcing stimulus. Thus a parent might be inadvertently developing new acquired reinforcers when she pairs natural displays of love and affection while she is reading to her toddler. In some remedial situations this consequent pairing procedure is used to help a child to develop reinforcing functions for social stimuli, such as "Well done," "Right," and "You're doing fine." At the beginning of training, which is referred to as a *percentage reinforcement schedule,* words and phrases of this sort are always paired (100%) with known reinforcers for the child. Then the frequency of pairing is systematically reduced (80%, 60%, 40%, etc.) so that in a relatively short period the words alone are effective, requiring only an occasional pairing with the known reinforcers.

Recall that the soundest way to determine whether a stimulus is a reinforcer is to test its effect on some operant response that precedes it or escapes it. Now we see that in many cases we can make a fair prediction about the reinforcing qualities of a stimulus. In general, whenever a stimulus has been discriminative for reinforcement, that stimulus will very likely (but not certainly) acquire a reinforcing property itself. It is still necessary to test it to be certain. But if investigation of the role a stimulus plays in the environment shows that it has been discriminative for reinforcement, then that stimulus is a probable candidate for testing as an acquired reinforcer.

It follows from this discussion that to transform a neutral stimulus into a reinforcing stimulus, some already effective reinforcer must be available first. Not all of the reinforcers that are effective for an individual can be acquired ones; some must have been effective from the beginning of psychological development. The term *primary reinforcer* often has been used to denote these original reinforcing stimuli. However, since relatively little is known about why primary reinforcers work, it is difficult to define them, other than to say that they seem to be reinforcing without a history to explain how they acquire their reinforcing power. For our purposes, we need only to discover what stimuli are effective reinforcers for infants at any moment in their development, and to trace changes. Whether these reinforcers are primary or acquired is not critical to the learning that will take place through their future role in the children's environments. Some of the important reinforcers that are probably primary and are thus basic to development include food, water, tactual stimuli, sucking-produced stimulation, taste stimuli, skin temperature, rest and sleep, the opportunity to breathe, and aversive stimuli (Bijou & Baer, 1965, pp. 86-107).

THE CONCEPT OF GENERALIZED REINFORCERS

We pointed out in Chapter 8 that when a stimulus becomes discriminative for a reinforcement occasion, generalization may be expected, that is, other stimuli, to the extent that they are similar to the discriminative stimulus, also take on discriminative functional properties. Because a discriminative stimulus is functionally equivalent to an acquired reinforcer, then just as the discriminative aspects of a stimulus generalize, so do its reinforcing characteristics. Therefore, we may legitimately refer to a generalized discriminative stimulus and to a generalized reinforcing stimulus as a generalized reinforcer. Unfortunately, the term generalized reinforcer is used differently in the behavioral psychology literature, referring to reinforcers that have acquired their function in another special way.

A *generalized reinforcer* owes its reinforcing property to a history of being paired with *several* reinforcing stimuli. Due to this multiple interactional history, the generalized reinforcer does not depend on one class of setting events to be effective; it is functional under a wide range of setting events. That is because it has been established as a reinforcer in the context of a variety of settings. For example, it may represent a stimulus discriminative for food, for water, and for shelter. Whereas it might be expected that a stimulus discriminative only for food would be effective only when food deprivation was in effect, a stimulus discriminative for food, water, and shelter ought to be effective in conditions of food deprivation, *or* of water deprivation, *or* of extremes of temperature. There are many more occasions, and a much wider range of events. Thus, to whatever extent setting events control the effectiveness of the stimulus, that stimulus ought to function more often than if it was not generalized in this manner. For instance, a mother's attention is a complex social stimulus that is discriminative for food and other (many of them social) reinforcers for her infant. Consequently, her attention serves as a generalized reinforcer. Other well-known examples include praise, approval, tokens, and money.

But a generalized reinforcer also generalizes. After a mother's attention becomes a generalized reinforcer, the attention of many other people (nurse, grandmother, baby sitter) also will reinforce the baby's operant behavior, almost as well as the mother's. It is obvious that an infant or a child can be controlled not only by the specific and generalized reinforcing stimuli provided by his parents, but also by those similar stimuli provided by others, such as school teachers and relatives.

DIFFERENCE BETWEEN ACQUIRED REINFORCING FUNCTION AND ACQUIRED ELICITING FUNCTION

A comparison of the acquired reinforcing function of a stimulus for operant behavior and the acquired eliciting function of a stimulus for respondent behavior will serve to clarify the similarities and differences between these two kinds of antecedent stimulus events. Procedurally, the two are similar. To endow a stimulus with an acquired eliciting function, we present a neutral stimulus just before a stimulus that already has eliciting value for some respondent (that is, we arrange a situation to produce respondent conditioning). To give a stimulus an acquired reinforcing operant function, we present a neutral stimulus on occasions when a stimulus that already has reinforcing property for an operant response is either presented or removed. The correlation of two stimulus events, one neutral and one reinforcing, is sometimes referred to in psychology as S-S (stimulus-stimulus) conditioning. However, we must remember certain differences between the respondent and operant interactions. For example, a stimulus that has acquired reinforcing property will be effective in influencing *any* other operants that precede it, or that remove it from an individual's environment.

SUMMARY OF OPERANT INTERACTIONS

We take this occasion to summarize the dynamics of operant interactions that have been presented in some detail in Chapters 5-9. To understand the occurrence or non-occurrence of an operant interaction, we should know at least the following:

1. The function of a stimulus consequent to a class of operant behaviors; namely, the presentation or removal of a positive or negative reinforcer, or of a neutral stimulus (pages 44-59).
2. The promptness with which the stimulus function is applied or has been applied in the past (pages 65-67).
3. The extent to which particular discriminative stimuli have accompanied this behavior and its stimulus consequences (pages 68-70).
4. The history of the stimulus function involved: whether it is a learned or unlearned reinforcer or a specific or generalized reinforcer; and, if learned, the details of the learning process (pages 90-94).
5. The number of times the behavior has in the past had similar stimulus consequence, that is, one with a similar stimulus function (pages 68-70).
6. The schedule according to which the behavior produces, removes, or avoids this or a similar stimulus consequence (pages 71-78).
7. The setting event for this interaction (pages 26-28).

REFERENCE

Bijou, S.W. and Baer, D.M., *Child Development: The Universal Stage of Infancy.* Vol. 2. Englewood Cliffs, N.J.: Prentice-Hall, 1965.

10

Complex Interactions: Conflict, Decision Making, Emotional and Affective Interactions

So far, we have analyzed operant and respondent interactions separately, emphasizing the differences in the dynamic principles of each. Without abridging the significance of these differences, we now make the transition to a more complex level of analysis, because in a child's everyday behavior both operant and respondent behaviors interact with each other in intricate ways. An understanding of these complex interactions requires that we observe simultaneously the effects of the operant behaviors on the respondents, and conversely, the effects of the respondents on the operant—in other words, the interactions of *multiple stimulus and multiple response functions.* It also requires that we take into account the fact that most complex interactions consist of a sequence with a number of operant-respondent sets called by various names, such as attending, perceiving, manipulating, effecting, and affecting. Each set serves a unique function in the sequence and the entire episode is designed with a label such as conflict or decision making.

Consider again the behavior of eating. A girl in a mild state of food deprivation goes into the kitchen and asks her mother for a cookie. The cookie is reinforcing, and the operant response ("Gimme a cookie") has been reinforced by cookies in past situations in which the mother (giver of cookies) has served as a cue (discriminative stimulus) for such a request. This is a very brief historical account of the child's behavior in relation to this situation. So far, the analysis has involved only operant principles. But there is more. We observed, during this episode, that as the child is given the cookie, she is likely to salivate. This interaction between the sight of the cookie and her mouth-watering response is a conditioned respondent. The taste of a cookie (like the taste of almost any food) serves as an unconditioned eliciting stimulus for the respondent of salivation. Although the *sight* of cookies once had no power to elicit salivation, it has, through its almost invariable association with the taste of cookies in the child's history, acquired eliciting power. The respondent of salivation has become conditioned to the sight of a cookie. Here, then, is one respondent interaction intertwined with the ongoing operant interaction of asking, obtaining, and chewing.

Furthermore, this respondent salivation inevitably provides stimulation to the child: she feels the increased salivation in her mouth, a stimulus that must have served as a cue on past occasions for putting the cookie in her mouth, which is a response reinforced by the ingestion of the cookies. Hence, the respondent provides the child with an added discriminative stimulus for continuing the series of operant responses. The sight of the cookie, the feel of it in her hand, and the feel of increased salivation are all discriminative stimuli for the response of putting the cookie in the mouth.

Swallowing and the resulting wave of peristaltic contractions of the child's esophagus which passes the chewed cookies down to the stomach is another example. The chain of operant behaviors starting with the child's request for the cookie ends in a long chain of respondents, starting with peristalsis and continuing with the internal responses making up the digestive process, all of which are respondents.

Some psychologists lose interest in the child's behavior at the point at which she puts the cookie in her mouth. The child has not stopped behaving toward the food; the psychologist has stopped behaving in relation to the child. In effect, the psychologist has arbitrarily stopped studying this complex chain of operant and respondent interactions at a point recognized as one of the rough boundaries of the field. The rest of the chain is left to be studied by physiologists and others (as noted in Chapter 2, pages 12-16). However, if the cookie were to cause the girl a stomach ache, which changes the course of his operant interactions, the psychologist might resume his interest. (Recall the discussion of organismic stimuli on page 22).

And finally, we may expect that a young child, given a cookie, will smile and laugh and will seem "pleased." These behaviors have a large respondent component which is a notable characteristic of this reinforcement situation. We may generalize from this example: most operant interactions will be intermixed with respondent interactions.

We diagram this operant-respondent sequence on the following page.

Let us consider another example involving food: a mother nursing her infant. The sight of the mother and her vocalizations are considered initially neutral social stimuli. But she is present on occasions when

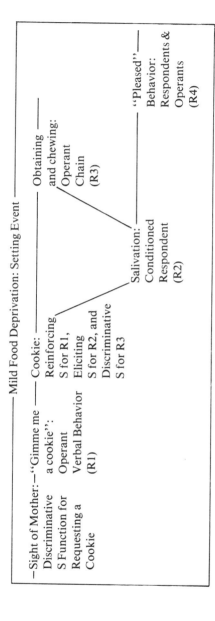

Figure 10-1

respondent behaviors are elicited and reinforcing stimuli are presented. The mother presents the eliciting stimulus of her nipple (or a bottle's nipple) for respondent sucking; she also provides milk, a positive reinforcer. Consequently, as a social stimulus, the mother should simultaneously acquire an eliciting function for sucking, and a reinforcing function for any of the baby's behavior. And, indeed, it is often observed that hungry infants do show anticipatory sucking when picked up by the mother (testifying to her acquired eliciting function), and also come to love the mother (testifying to her acquired reinforcing function). Diagramatically, this analysis is as follows:

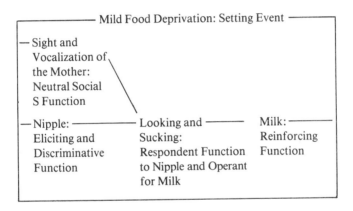

Let us take a third example, one involving electric shock as an aversive stimulus. Putting your finger in a live electric socket produces respondent behaviors (muscle contraction in the shocked part of the body, and perhaps a sudden gasp, and a vocalization such as "Ouch!"). Electric shock also acts as a punishing stimulus and a negative reinforcer, weakening operants that produce it, and strengthening operants that reduce, escape, or avoid it. Then the neutral stimulus presented immediately before the onset of electric shock (sight of the electric socket) simultaneously may acquire eliciting *and* reinforcing powers. It may have eliciting power over some of the respondents that the shock itself elicits (mild contraction in the finger and tenseness) and reinforcing power over any operants that reduce, remove, or avoid it (looking away when an electric socket is in view). Diagrammatically, this interaction looks like this:

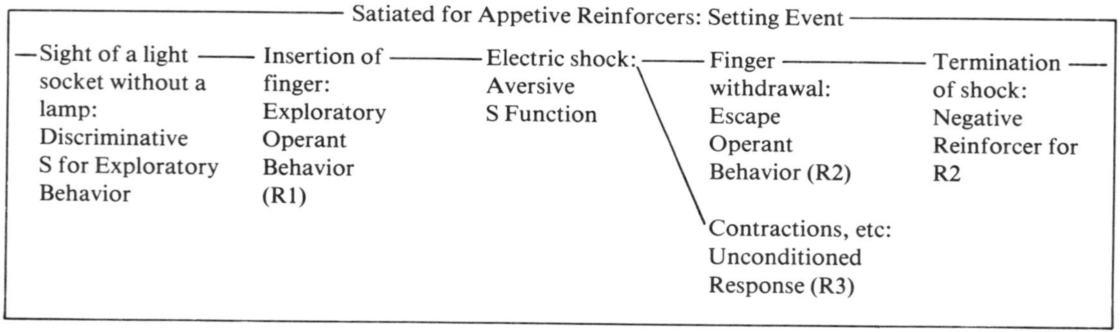

Satiated for Appetive Reinforcers: Setting Event

— Sight of a light socket without a lamp: Discriminative S for Exploratory Behavior

— Insertion of finger: Exploratory Operant Behavior (R1)

— Electric shock: Aversive S Function

— Finger withdrawal: Escape Operant Behavior (R2)

Contractions, etc: Unconditioned Response (R3)

— Termination of shock: Negative Reinforcer for R2

Figure 10-2

CONFLICT: INCOMPATIBLE STIMULUS AND RESPONSE FUNCTIONS

Operant and respondent interactions do not always operate harmoniously or augment each other as in the previous examples. Consider now the situations that produce two or more stimulus consequences with opposing, contradictory, or conflictive reinforcing functions.

Situations in which there is conflict because response consequences lead to opposing stimulus functions:

1. An operant may at the same time produce both a positive and a negative reinforcer. The first stimulus function strengthens the operant, the second weakens it. A teacher commenting, "Good, you did that example correctly" (positive reinforcement), "Now devote the rest of the recess period to finishing the next five examples" (negative reinforcement).

2. An operant may produce a positive reinforcer and simultaneously lose or avoid a positive reinforcer. The first stimulus function strengthens the response, the second weakens it. Receiving money (positive reinforcer) in exchange for one of an artist's prized paintings (losing a positive reinforcer).

3. An operant may produce a negative reinforcer and simultaneously avoid another negative reinforcer. The first stimulus function weakens the operant; the second strengthens it. Jumping out of a window of a burning house (avoiding negative reinforcement) and breaking an arm in the fall (producing a negative reinforcer).

4. An operant may lose a positive reinforcer and simultaneously avoid or escape a negative reinforcer. The first stimulus function weakens the response, the second strengthens it. A speeding motorist paying a fine (losing a positive reinforcer) rather than going to jail (avoiding a negative reinforcer).

5. An operant may at different times produce contradictory stimulus consequences. A response may be positively reinforcing immediately but negatively reinforcing later. "Fly now, pay later" is one such application. Having "just one more" at a cocktail party and getting sick later is another. On the other hand, a response may be negatively reinforcing immediately but positively reinforcing later. Taking a cold shower on arising so as to feel good for the rest of the morning.

6. The functions of discriminative stimuli may signal occasions for later contradictory reinforcement. The girl who watches TV when

she should be studying is receiving positive reinforcement (the TV program) at the moment, but she is not failing her test at the same time—that reinforcement event will probably occur the next day. However, she is in the presence of a discriminative stimulus indicating an occasion for negative reinforcement (test failure) the next day. Remember that discriminative stimuli function as acquired reinforcers (pages 90-93). Thus a conflict between opposing discriminative stimuli is, in this sense, a conflict between reinforcers present *at the moment.*

7. The discriminative stimuli present may be unclear or confused because of a person's history of reinforcement in the presence of these stimuli. When someone calls you an idiot, but smiles as he says it, are you being positively or negatively reinforced? If you have never before experienced this combination of stimuli, you may be in a conflict: "Does he really think I'm an idiot or is he teasing me?"

DECISION MAKING

What happens when a response has consequences that simultaneously act to weaken and strengthen it, or when contradictory or ambiguous discriminative stimuli are presented? The answer is implicit in the summary list of the seven situations presented above: we must assess the strength of each stimulus function and its power to affect the operant, and then compare the strengths of the opposing functions. How is the strength of a stimulus function assessed? It is assessed largely by the details that comprise the situations.

This prescription is the common sense answer to decision making. When caught between the devil and the deep blue sea, you ask yourself or others some pertinent questions before making a choice. "How dangerous is the devil? How hot is his fire? What is my present temperature? How cold is the deep blue sea? How good am I at swimming? How far is it to shore?"

A child's everyday life contains many situations in which opposing stimulus functions are unavoidable and decisions have to be made. For example, consider the boy who has been told that he will get $3 for cutting the grass, which must be cut today, and then discovers that his gang is having an important baseball game today with a rival team. In this illustration there are at least two operants, each of which has opposing stimulus consequences. The boy may cut the grass. This response earns him $3, a definite positive reinforcer, but loses him participation in the ball game, a loss of both fun and approval from his peers, which are positive social reinforcers. The $3 should promote grass-cutting; the loss of fun and approval from peers should weaken it. On the other hand, the boy may go to the game. In this case, he has lots of fun and gets peer approval, but does not get the $3. Besides, when he gets home he will probably encounter his parents' angry disapproval, and perhaps lose other reinforcers, such as his allowance or other privileges. The fun and peer approval should promote ball playing, but the loss of the money, the parental disapproval, and the potential loss of other reinforcers should weaken ball playing.

To find out what decision the boy will make, we need a great deal of information about him and his situation. In fact, we need exactly the kind of information summarized in outline form at the end of Chapter 9. For example: one basic reinforcer involved is the $3. What is his deprivation condition for dollars? What does the boy mean to buy with it? What is his deprivation state for that? Peer approval is another basic reinforcer involved here. What is the boy's deprivation state for this stimulus? What is his usual schedule of peer approval as a reinforcer? How powerful is the parental approval that can compete with peer approval? What is its schedule? Its deprivation state? Its history of acquisition?

The answers to these and similar questions obviously contribute to a sort of bookkeeping of debits and credits for the stimulus functions involved. The final answer, or decision, will follow from an adding up of the plus and minus factors for each response, to see which will control the operant. An important problem for psychology, clearly, is to devise methods of measuring or scaling factors such as these in ways that permit assigning numbers to them.

However, the point to emphasize here is that conflict and decision making are not special topics requiring new principles. The principles involved are the same as those in simpler operant situations, except that they are applied to complex combinations. The accounting required may be difficult, but it is not impossible, in principle, and the values for all the terms can be lawfully determined.

Two considerations make conflict and decision making important interactions. The first is the possibility, at least in theory, of finding a conflict situation in which the opposing stimulus functions exactly balance each other, so that the case tending to strengthen an operant is exactly as powerful as the case tending to weaken it. Then, we may observe a child vacillating between the alternatives, choosing first the one, then the other, and neither for very long. The boy in our previous example might, if the stimuli were exactly balanced, start cutting the grass, then after a few minutes give it up, get his baseball glove, and start for the baseball field. Halfway there he might stop, mutter to himself, and head back home to cut some more grass. After some vigorous mower-pushing, he might again pick up his glove, go to the game, and actually play a couple of innings. (As he sees it, with the grass half cut, the parental disapproval he is risking may be less severe than if none of the grass were cut.) If he continues to play for a few more innings, and his team is well ahead now, the possibility of earning $3 and getting his parents' approval might prove reinforcing enough to start him home again to finish the grass. (He has had some fun and his peers probably will not disapprove of him for leaving when the game seems won anyway.) Thus, in special instances, conflict can produce a back-and-forth set of decisions which, at first glance, may seem like a special kind of response, unlike anything discussed so far. However, such behavior is readily explained by the principles that explain operant behaviors in general. Each sub-decision alters the strengths of the functional properties of the stimuli, responses, and setting events, and destroys the balance between the alternatives.

The second point about conflict and decision making, which might make them seem a special problem, is this: when the child is placed in a situation where a response will have stimulus consequences with opposing functions, he may show "emotional" behavior. That is, we say that he seems "frustrated" or "torn" by the conflict, or, more loosely, "hung up." Much of this follows from the fact that very often in conflict situations the child must make a decision that accepts negative reinforcement in order to get more powerful positive reinforcement, or loses positive reinforcement in order to escape or avoid more powerful negative reinforcement. The occurrence of negative reinforcers, or the loss of positive reinforcers, has a close connection with what is popularly called "emotional" behavior, the topic we will consider next. The point to stress here is that conflict and decision making are analyzed in terms of the principles we have discussed in Chapters 3 through 9 and are not new subject matters.

EMOTIONAL INTERACTIONS

Emotion is a term fraught with difficulties when it is approached scientifically. The first problem is that emotion is a noun, and as such conveys the expression that it is a thing. In Chapter 1, we stated that behavioral psychology does not deal with things, but rather with the interactions between the behavior of an individual and his environment. The second problem is that emotion is a term that has been heavily influenced by cultural beliefs and attitudes. Even the pioneer behaviorist, John B. Watson (1919), accepted the popular notion that the basic emotions—fear, anger, and love—could be put in good scientific order by considering them instincts, the fountainhead of all complex emotions.

We shall (1) analyze the popular meaning of emotion according to the operant and respondent interactions involved, (2) comment on the venerable James-Lange theory of emotion, and (3) present Kantor's formulation, the one we believe to be consistent with the natural science approach.

Popular Conceptions

Emotional behavior, as it is referred to in everyday conversation, generally refers to respondent interactions. But in these complex interactions, the eliciting stimuli for respondent behavior may have reinforcing properties for operant behaviors. The reverse is also true. In many situations reinforcing a child by any of the procedures previously discussed (see Table 1, page 52) may also elicit respondent behavior. Consider these examples:

1. A boy described in his presence as "still wetting the bed" may blush. Here, blushing is a respondent interaction elicited by the presentation of a conditioned negative reinforcer (disapproval). In lay language, we say that the child is "ashamed."

2. A girl wakes up Christmas morning, runs to the tree, and discovers the bicycle she has wanted for over a year. She may break into goose pimples, flush, and breathe faster. A layman might say that she is "thrilled." The respondents here are elicited by the sudden presentation of a positive reinforcer that is very powerful because of a prolonged period of deprivation.

3. Take a cookie away from a baby. Loud cries and tears are likely almost immediately. These are respondent behaviors elicited by the sudden removal of a positive reinforcer. We might say that the baby is "angry."

4. A mother tells her nine-year-old daughter that she need not wash the dishes tonight. Perhaps the girl will smile, giggle, and whoop as she dashes off. We might say that she is "relieved" by the unexpected removal of a negative reinforcer.

5. A mother has locked the recreation room door because there is

broken glass on the floor. A girl wanting her puzzle box reaches for the knob, turns it, and pushes, but cannot open the door. She may then tug violently at the knob, kick the door, cry, and shout. Such interactions are clearly operant but they may also involve several respondents that are elicited because an operant previously reinforced every time it occurred in the child's history with door knobs is for the first time not being reinforced. That is to say, her turning and pushing on the knob is not resulting in the reinforcers heretofore provided by opening the door and getting her toys on the other side. We might say that the child is "frustrated"—but we can claim only that she is displaying certain respondents correlated with the failure of reinforcement to occur.

These examples demonstrate that any of the basic reinforcement and extinction procedures discussed in Chapter 5 may at the same time elicit respondent behaviors. These respondents are popularly labeled "emotional" mainly because of the situations that give rise to them. When a hot room leads to dilation of the blood vessels on the surface of the skin, and a child becomes flushed, we do not say that the child is emotional; yet when a scolding leads to the same dilation of the same blood vessels, we may indeed say that the child is blushing with shame and hence is emotional. The respondent has not changed, but the situation has. In the popular sense, then, emotional behaviors are respondent interactions in relation to particular kinds of eliciting stimulation, usually to positive or negative reinforcing stimuli being presented or removed, or to the beginning of extinction.

In the preceding section on conflict, the final point was that conflict often seemed to have a distinctively emotional component—being "torn" by conflict. We see now that much of the emotional behavior in conflict requires that in order to endure or resolve a conflict, one must either accept negative reinforcement (perhaps to get more positive reinforcement) or must lose positive reinforcement (perhaps to avoid more negative reinforcement). Such interactions, described in the examples above, elicit respondent behaviors. Furthermore, in conflict situations where the values of the opposing reinforcers are nearly equal, so that children oscillate between one response and another, often they cannot do anything else until they make their decision. Since there may be many other discriminative stimuli present for other behaviors with other reinforcing contingencies, and since these are not being responded to, additional emotional behavior may be generated. Consider the girl asked to go to a dance who cannot decide which of two dresses to wear. As she stands before her closet, temporarily incapable of choosing between the two garments, time is passing—a discriminative stimulus requiring many other responses, such as putting on her cosmetics, if she is going to avoid the negative reinforcement of being late. But the stimulus of time passing cannot be responded to, perhaps, until she settles on one dress. If each dress has an equal reinforcing value to her, we would expect that the situation will stall her and elicit flurries of irritation and other respondents.

James-Lange Theory

It is sometimes argued that reinforcers affect behavior the way they do *because* of the emotional response they elicit; that ultimately it is the emotion that is powerful and that the reinforcer is effective only because it elicits emotional respondent behavior, which generates internal stimulation ("feelings"). William James' famous example (1890) explaining why we run from bears can clarify this kind of reasoning. Usually, it is argued that we run from a bear because we are afraid of it; by running, we escape from the source of our fear. In other words, the bear acts as a negative reinforcer *because* it makes us afraid. James offered an alternative argument which has become known as the James-Lange theory: we run from a bear (a negative reinforcer), and are afraid *because* we are *running.* We can diagram these two possibilities, and a third, which is a useful alternative, in the following way:

1. Usual argument: *Bear* causes *fear* which causes *running.*
2. James' argument: *Bear* causes *running* which causes *fear.*
3. Alternative: *Bear is a discriminative stimulus* for running operants that escape from the bear (a conditioned negative reinforcer). Also an *eliciting stimulus* for fear respondents.

This argument probably cannot be settled. Perhaps emotions explain reinforcement effects; perhaps reinforcement effects explain emotions. We shall say only that the two often go hand-in-hand, without assigning a cause-and-effect relationship. Let it be argued that we see bears and run because bears are discriminative stimuli for negative reinforcement (and therefore are themselves acquired negative reinforcers); *at the same time,* we are fearful because bears are acquired negative reinforcers, and the presentation of negative reinforcers is a conditioned stimulus situation eliciting the respondents said to make up "fear" (the third alternative above). One thing is certain: we often may observe reinforcing stimuli interacting with behavior in their usual manner, yet we find no objective evidence of emotional respondent behaviors. This kind of observation is responsible for much research that concentrates on operant interactions. As scientists, we must rely as much as possible on *observable* stimulus and response events. When we can observe reinforcing stimuli interacting with behaviors, and cannot observe emotional respondents intertwined with the behaviors, we tend to lean primarily on operant rather than respondent principles for analysis and explanation.

Kantor's Formulation

Kantor views emotion, or an emotional interaction, as *a momentary cessation of operant behavior on the occasion of a sudden change in the environment* (Kantor, 1966 and Kantor & Smith, 1975, pp. 239-252). His analysis consists of five distinct phases:

1. The interactions are in progress prior to the sudden change in the environment (baseline). Using an example similar to the bear-in-the-woods, let us say that on a warm spring day you wander away from your picnicking friends and go strolling in the woods, humming, "When the saints go marching in," and admiring the blossoms, birds, and wild flowers. The manner and pace of your walking and your humming and interactions with the flora describe your operant baseline behaviors. If you were wired for remote biomonitoring, like an astronaut, the activities of your vital organs and systems, such as respiration, would describe your respondent baseline behavior.

2. There is sudden change in the environment (the emotionalizing event). All at once a large, black, menacing bear appears before you.

3. The cessation of operant interactions and changes in respondent interactions take place (the emotional reaction). You abruptly stop walking, humming, and exploring. All of your operant behavior is at a standstill; you "freeze" momentarily. At this time, the remote-control biomonitoring system shows drastic changes in your biological functioning.

4. The operant interactions follow the cessation of operant interactions (recovery). After a brief period, you spin around and run as fast as you can in the other direction. The operant behavior of running at top speed has replaced the operant behaviors of strolling, humming, and browsing, and the respondent behaviors change

further in synchronization with the new strenuous operant behavior (breathing increases, adrenal output increases, etc.).

5. The predispositions for operant and respondent behaviors persist for a period after recovery (organismic setting event, see page 28). Back among your picnicking friends, you calm down and relate your harrowing experience. After giving your account (perhaps several times) you rant against the park department's neglect for the safety of the public and you are hostile to anyone who defends the park department's services (predisposition to engage in aggressive behavior). At the same time you keep an active lookout for indications that the bear is in the vicinity and are sensitive ("jumpy") to sudden changes. Furthermore, you interpret your best friend's joke about its being better to see a bear than a pink elephant as a deliberate attempt to make you feel bad (predisposition to react to aversive stimuli, a kind of a temporary paranoia).

Clearly, then, this behavioral concept of emotion is not simply that of a set of certain respondents that occur in certain situations, nor simply a pattern of respondent and operant behaviors. It is, rather, a momentary cessation of ongoing operant behavior on the occasion of a sudden environmental change and takes into account the pre-emotional behavior, the sudden environmental change, the cessation of numerous and various operants and changes in respondents, and the recovery and predispositional phases. There are, of course, differences in emotional interactions in the sense of differences in intensity, from mild emotions, such as "embarrassment" for a social *faux pas,* to severe ones, such as a serious threat to one's life.

AFFECTIVE INTERACTIONS

Does this formulation of emotional interaction ignore what are commonly considered the basic emotions, such as fear, love, rage, and anger? It does, but many of the behaviors included in these terms are analyzed as *affective interaction.* (Kantor, 1966, & Kantor and Smith, 1975.) Affective interactions are a class of interrelated operant and respondent behaviors described in the first section of this chapter that are a part of extinction (frustration, anger, hostility), removal of strong, generalized, social discriminative stimuli (loneliness, grief, homesickness), strong natural or acquired aversive stimuli (anxiety, fear), natural or acquired powerful positive reinforcing stimuli (joy, happiness, pleasure, love), and strong setting events, such as extreme deprivation of reinforcing stimuli, drugs, and physical damage (delusions, delirium, euphoria, and hallucinations).

Affective behavior may be distinguished from effective behavior (the kind described in most of the examples in the preceding chapters) in terms of the *locus of stimuli acted on in an interactional sequence:* affective behavior is directed toward internal stimuli, effective behavior toward external stimuli. A mother hearing that her child was killed in a car accident would probably engage in severe forms of *affective* behavior, such as crying, holding her head, secluding herself and saying over and over again, "It's not true." After a while, she might engage in relevant *effective* behavior, such as calling the police to find out where the child's body is and obtaining further information about the accident.

Of course, affective and effective behaviors can occur at the same time. While the mother is engaging in the effective behavior of calling to find out the details of the accident, she is in all probability still engaging in the kinds of affective behavior associated with the sudden loss of a loved one. Under these circumstances, the affective interaction functions as an organismic setting event influencing some of the characteristics of the effective interaction. In this case it might be halting and repetitious speech that might be described as conflict (pages 101-102). Thus an affective interaction is similar to an emotional interaction in that both have a *predispositional* component (see page 109).

REFERENCES

JAMES, W., *The Principles of Psychology*. Vol. 2. New York: Henry Holt and Co., 1890, 149-150.

KANTOR, J.R., Feelings and emotions as scientific events. *Psychological Record*, 1966, *16*, 377-404.

KANTOR, J.R. AND SMITH, N.W., *The Science of Psychology: An Interbehavioral Survey*. Chicago: Principia Press, 1975, pp. 222-238.

WATSON, J.B., *Psychology from the Standpoint of a Behavioralist*. Philadelphia: J.B. Lippincott, 1919.

11

Complex Interactions: Self-Management, Biofeedback, Problem Solving, Thinking, and Creativity

Complex interactions also include self-management interactions, biofeedback control, problem solving, thinking, and creativity. These are interactions in which children respond in ways that alter their environments, that is, change the functional properties of the acting stimuli or setting events, and thereby influence the course of their own interactions.

SELF-MANAGEMENT

We begin our discussion of self-management with the reminder that part of a child's environment is inside the skin (see page 21). For example, a mother may take her little son to a department store at Christmas time. On the way through the toy department, the boy will be deluged with discriminative stimuli marking the occasion for thousands of possible responses (play) with hundreds of possible reinforcers (toys). As the mother lets go of her child's hand to turn a price tag, the boy moves off toward a toy counter and reaches for a particularly alluring gadget. Just as his hand is about to touch it, we *may* hear him quietly saying over and over his mother's thousand-times-repeated admonition, "DON'T TOUCH!" Consequently his hand retreats slowly, and he stands there, gazing sadly at the toy. The boy is in momentary conflict. Here, two sets of responses—one related to stimuli from the external environment (toys) and one to stimuli from the internal environment resulting in admonishing verbal behavior—have occurred in succession with the second set influencing (terminating the initial stages of reaching) the first set.

Stimuli from internal sources, verbal and nonverbal, may influence responses of the same individual in many ways. A real-estate agent may talk to himself about infuriating memories of the city council's decision on zone restriction (occasions when positive reinforcers were lost or negative reinforcers were presented) that produce respondents which in turn bolster his operant behavior sufficiently to start an argument or a fight. A boy may wake in the middle of the night and say, "I don't have to ask to go to the potty," and then leave his bedroom for the bathroom. Without this self-generated reassurance, a child who is usually scolded or spanked for getting up after being put to bed might not get up, and would call the sleeping parents instead. If they failed to hear that call, the child might wet the bed. A child may say again and again, "If I'm good today, Daddy will take me to the playground after dinner," and this reaction to his own behavior may actually prevent some of the usual daily misbehaviors. Another example is the self-management of overeating (Stuart and Davis, 1972). Basically, eating is a food-reinforced behavior, and many persons reach a satiation point for food only after they have ingested too many calories to maintain a steady weight. Becoming overweight as indicated by a scale or tight clothes is a stimulus event that occurs long after the response causing it (overeating); hence this presumed negative reinforcer is not effective in weakening the overeating behavior (and so does not rate the term of negative reinforcer for this behavior). Generally, only through techniques of self-management can overweight persons reduce. They must make eating an occasion for other behaviors that may immediately punish overeating or that strengthen some competitive response; or they must otherwise reduce the powerful reinforcing property of food. One instance of such self-management is making eating the occasion for verbal behavior equating food to calories and calories to pounds: "This piece of banana cream pie contains about 500 calories. That's more than one-third of my total calorie allowance for the day, which means that if I eat it, I'll probably gain weight rather than lose weight today." Words of this sort can add an immediate negative reinforcer to the tempting situation, which is escaped from by eating less and foregoing favorite foods (or by "forgetting" to say the words!). Many other possibilities have the same effect, such as substituting low-calorie foods for rich foods. A final example of self-management, and one not involving verbal behavior, is the college student who drinks vast quantities of coffee to counteract sleepiness the night before a test. Coffee drinking makes prolonged studying possible.

A particularly interesting aspect of self-management is the development of "conscience" in children. The ability of a child to behave in moral ways as taught, *in the absence of parents and teachers,* has been a critical problem in personality development throughout the history of child psychology. Explanations accounting for such self-managing behavior have given rise to theories with hypothetical internal determiners, such as the self or the super-ego, and hypothetical processes, such as the internalization of parents' standards.

We sometimes see a little girl misbehaving, and even as she is doing what she has been told not to do, cheerfully saying, "No, no, no, no." However, with the child's further development, the "No, no, no, no" becomes less cheerful, precedes the misbehavior, and often prevents it. Why? An analysis of her interactional history might reveal this kind of background information: When she has committed a misdeed previously—let us say taking her mother's stationery from the desk to scribble on—her mother has taken it away from her and said, "No, no." If she has had little history with "No, no" as a signal for punishment, its stimulus function for her is an indication of her mother's attention, a positive social reinforcer. The simple "No, no," without any accompanying punishment, is a verbalization marking occasions of positive social reinforcement, and as a consequence, takes on a positive reinforcing property itself. Hence the verbal behavior (sounds) that produces it (the child using her own vocal apparatus to say "No, no") is strengthened, since similar sounds made by her mother have been paired with positive social reinforcement. However, a child at the toddler stage of development is likely to be doing many things all day long that lead the mother to say "No, no" repeatedly as she stops the girl and rescues valuables or rescues the child from danger. Naturally, the mother will probably take a stricter and stricter role in trying to modify the child's misbehavior into acceptable forms. Her "No, no" becomes a discriminative stimulus for repeated punishments, both through the presentation of negative reinforcers and the withdrawal of positive reinforcers. Thus, "No, no" begins to change its stimulus function for the child: as it becomes more and more clearly a discriminative stimulus for punishment, it is transformed into a social negative reinforcer, rather than a social positive reinforcer. As the child herself says "No, no" on future occasions of investigating her mother's stationery, she is providing her own punishment or her own cues for potential punishment, and her behavior weakens accordingly.

This analysis demonstrates that there is no need for a special principle to analyze the development of "conscience." The self-generated behaviors that prevent bad behavior and promote good behavior can readily be analyzed in terms of the principles presented. An investigation of children's histories of specific interactions can show that they learn to manage themselves by saying "No, no" in the same way that they learn all their other operant behavior: through the action of reinforcement contingencies in which "No, no" is a verbal operant, strengthened typically by social reinforcement from parents, teachers, and others.

However, the concept of self-management often tempts the theorist to invoke special principles because the "self" is generally thought to be something that acts on its own, has volition and will, and is different from all the interactions of the individual. Self-management is a chain of interactions in which the changes are brought about in stimulus functions. The early parts of the chain influence interactions in the later parts and therefore the behavior is subject to the kinds of stimulus events that affect other operant interactions. *Self-management is defined as the control of certain responses by stimuli generated from other responses of the same individual, that is, by self-generated stimuli.* If these self-generated stimuli are not observable, it is easy to attribute the observed behavior to unobservables. In the example of the boy in the store who reaches for a toy but stops short of picking it up, what if we do not hear him say "Don't touch" as he withdraws his hand? The inclination is to infer that some response-produced stimulation occurs internally that connects the observed response with some part of the child's history of learning that is relevant to the response. A behavior analysis approach repudiates this kind of inference. If observable responses produce observable stimuli that functionally relate to other behaviors, then we can talk about self-management by describing the functional relationships involved. If any of the critical responses or response-produced stimuli are not observable, application of the concept of self-management is totally unprofitable and dangerous in the sense of producing false knowledge.

Fortunately, much of the developing self-management behavior, in particular verbal behavior, of young children is observable. Young children frequently maintain a running conversation with themselves (Stone and Church, 1973), part of which is recognized by parents as exact quotations from their own admonitions to their children. More than one child has been observed to get up from a fall, wailing, "You should be more careful!" When such cautionary reminders occur earlier and earlier in play sequences, they can inhibit careless behavior and stimulate careful play behavior.

Although these examples are common, they are by no means universal in young children. To the extent that they exist in observable forms, instances of conscience and similar behaviors may be analyzed objectively in behavioral terms. To the extent that such interactions are *not* observable, these concepts cannot be applied by a natural science approach to child development. This constraint may impose a limitation on a study of conscience in children, because many behaviors of this type may be mediated by internal responses not observable to the psychologist in the present state of our technology. However, an internal response is not necessarily an unobservable response. As research in physiological psychology advances, present techniques for observing internal stimulation and behavior will be improved. Present limitations to a study of internal "mediating" events may, therefore, be temporary. A natural science approach to psychological development is not restricted to stimulus and response interaction *outside* the organism; it applies to observable stimulus and response interactions wherever they occur.[1]

If internal responses in self-management are not observable, they still may be present and involved in self-managing; on the other hand, they may not exist at all. We cannot insist that internal self-managing interactions exist simply because a child behaves morally. Many principles of behavior, stated in terms of observable past interactions, could explain why certain "good" responses are strong, and other "bad" responses are weak. The point to emphasize in this approach is that we analyze behavior in terms of the conditions that are observable or potentially observable, rather than to say that a single mechanism such as self-management is responsible for early moral development, and we resort to potentially verifiable inferences about antecedent conditions when they cannot be observed directly.

A final example of self-management, and incidentally one that illustrates the interrelationship between operant and respondent behavior, relates to training an individual to win the $100 bet on the pupillary response, given in the discussion of respondent interactions (page 35). The contention earlier was that since the pupillary response is respondent behavior, it cannot be controlled by consequent reinforcing stimulation—not even by the offer of $100; that it can be elicited only by preceding stimulation. Let us prepare a friend to win the bet through her own operant behavior by giving her a conditioned eliciting stimulus which she may present to herself. First we condition her pupillary responses to a sound, by the usual procedure of respondent conditioning: we make the sound, and immediately shine a bright light in her eyes. The bright light elicits the pupillary response, and the sound, associated with the bright light, will by itself come to elicit the pupillary response, if we repeat this procedure

---

[1]Readers may study (react to) their own internal processes. *We* may not know anything about them, other than what *they* tell us. We cannot assume that what they tell us is simply a description of the internal processes. Our best assumption is that the verbal account is a function of (1) self reactions to internal processes, (2) the context or setting event, and (3) the listener or listeners.

often enough. For our particular purpose, we will use for the sound a spoken word, say "constrict." Past studies suggest that we may well succeed. As a consequence of this training, her pupils will constrict whenever she hears the word "constrict." She can now control one of her own respondent responses (pupillary) by her own operant behavior (saying "constrict"). Should an unwary psychologist offer $100 (reinforcer) if she can control a respondent such as the pupillary response (as an example of its insensitivity to consequence stimulation), the psychologist will lose as our friend calls out "constrict" and her pupils constrict.

A second, and somewhat simpler, technique is to inform our friend that looking from a near point of fixation to a far away point affects the pupillary response. A change in visual fixation, in fact, manipulates the eliciting stimulation that controls the pupillary response. To give her this information is to provide her with a chain of verbal operant responses, which, put to use on a later occasion, causes her to change her gaze (another operant), thus affecting the eliciting stimulation of light falling on the retina, which again will cost the psychologist $100 as it elicits the pupillary respondent.

In both techniques of self-management, we make it possible for an individual to use operant behavior that manipulates eliciting stimuli which control respondent behavior. In effect, by strengthening the critical operants (saying "constrict" or memorizing the principle about the change in visual fixation and the pupillary response), we furnish our friend with techniques of self-management. It should be emphasized, however, that when she engages in such self-management practices, *her behavior is still the consequence of her history of interaction and the present situation.*

BIOFEEDBACK

Instructing or training a person to control specific classes of his respondent interactions has in recent years proven to be serious business for many in need of treatment. Research in physiological psychology, largely pioneered by Miller (1969), has demonstrated that an individual who is suffering from glandular, visceral, or brain dysfunctioning can be relieved of pain or discomfort by "visceral learning" or biofeedback techniques. For example, an individual having high blood pressure and suffering severe migraine headaches can be relieved by training him, under laboratory conditions, how to lower his blood pressure by operant procedures. Since changes in blood pressure are internal respondent interactions, apparatus that visually or auditorially presents changes in this activity (e.g., the movement of a dial needle) is required. With such a device, indications (discriminative stimuli) of lowered blood pressure are reinforced in any way that is functional for the individual, indications that blood pressure is being lowered are reinforced, and indications that it is being raised are either not reinforced or are punished. This procedure has proven effective in many instances, even though the individual does not know "what he does" to bring about the desired change.

Another example is the use of operant procedures to influence brain wave patterns or sequences of electrical discharges recorded by an apparatus (polygraph) producing an electroencephalogram (EEG). Ordinarily there is little purpose in attempting to alter the frequencies of brain waves, but if changes in the frequency of a certain kind of wave precedes a disturbance, such as a seizure, then manipulation may be therapeutically worthwhile. This is true in certain types of epilepsy. It has been demonstrated that when specified classes of brain waves occur in higher frequencies, it is highly probable that within a short time the individual will have an epileptic attack. Epilepsy-prone individuals can be shown their own brain wave records as the polygraphy writes them, taught to identify the critical type of brain waves, and be given differential reinforcement training to decrease the occurrences of these frequencies. As in the self-management of high blood pressure, individuals may not know "what they do" to influence changes in their patterns of EEG's.

Although a large number of studies have demonstrated that internal processes can be conditioned through an antecedent link with operant interactions, it is too early to say how practical these techniques will be for the treatment of diverse types of physiological disorders. A great deal of research still needs to be done to authenticate the generality of findings, the effects of other conditions, the clinical significance of findings to date, the effect of biofeedback relative to other treatment techniques, and the maintenance of changes after termination of treatment.

PROBLEM SOLVING AND PRODUCTIVE THINKING

A mildly food-deprived young girl eyeing a glass cookie jar on a high kitchen shelf faces a problem if she cannot figure out how to reach that shelf and get a cookie. She looks around the room, sees a chair, moves it beneath the shelf, stands on it, reaches the jar, opens it, gets a cookie, and eats it. This is an example of a *problem solving*—a simple one, to be sure. It involves a situation in which a child cannot make an immediate response to reduce the setting event, such as mild deprivation of reinforcing stimuli (get a cookie from the jar on a high shelf), and sets about to alter the situation (move a chair to the shelf to stand on) and thereby increase the probability of a reinforceable response (reaching the jar, opening it, and getting a cookie). We diagram the operant part of the solving situation as follows:

─────────── Mild Food Deprivation: Setting Event ───────────				
─Sight of Jar ───── with Cookies on Shelf: Discriminative S Function for Problem-Solving Behavior	Surveying ─── Situation, Moving Chair and Standing on It: Operant Chain (R1)	Altered ─── Situation: Reinforcing S for R1 and Discriminative S for R2	Reaching,─── Opening Jar, and Getting a Cookie: Operant Chain(R2)	Cookie in ───── Mouth: Reinforcing S Function for R2 and Discriminative S Function for Next Response

Figure 11-1

The same analysis could be made for problem solving centering on escape from or avoidance of aversive stimuli (e.g., how to get out of an unbearably hot room upon discovering that the door is locked).

The altering-the-situation phase of problem solving may involve primarily (1) physical objects and events (the girl moving a chair and standing on it to get a cookie), or (2) social variables (putting words and sentences together in a way to convey "bad" news to someone without arousing a stong emotional reaction), or (3) personal conditions (restricting eating to three small meals a day to lose weight), or (4) abstractions (transposing numbers and signs to solve an algebra problem). Most problems include a combination of these interactions. The behaviors that are required for the solution must, of course, be in a child's repertory; the learning history must have included situations that developed the required responses, for otherwise the problem is insolvable. The child in our example must be able to conceptualize the chair as an object to stand on in order to extend her reach, and she must be physically able to move the chair beneath the shelf and to stand on it to solve the problem, at least in that way. Lacking this particular behavior repertory, she may have to solve the problem differently. She may, for example, slide the jar off the shelf with a broom handle as she has seen her mother do, and, if she is lucky, catch it before it crashes to the floor.

Problem solving resembles some forms of moral behavior or behavior guided by conscience. In moral behavior, the individual engages in interactions that increase the probabilities of good behaviors and decrease the probabilities of bad behaviors. In problem solving the interactions are apt to increase the occurrence of a response that solves the problem, that is, makes it possible to reach a goal in the form of an object, or an activity.

We have seen that problem solving situations may range from trivial to momentous; problem solving behaviors, from quick and easy to prolonged and deliberate; problem solving solutions, from common to unusual; and problem solving activities from completely overt to completely covert. In our girl-and-cookie-jar example, problem solving was almost entirely overt (looking around the room, seeing the chair, pushing it into place, standing on it, etc.). A different problem situation might bring about altering behavior that would be partially covert and partially overt. Had the kitchen been devoid of objects on which the child could stand to reach the cookie jar, she might stop a minute and *recall* where she last saw a suitable object, and, if manageable, bring it into the kitchen.

Productive Thinking

When the altering aspect of problem solving is primarily covert, problem solving is generally described as *productive thinking*. (The modifier "productive" is generally used to distinguish problem solving thinking from "free-association" thinking as in reverie or day dreaming.) Covert activity of this sort may be verbal, or nonverbal behavior, or a combination of both, and has the same properties as overt behavior. If it has any special properties they are speed and confidentiality (Skinner, 1974). Because of limited verbal repertories, preschool children's problem solving behaviors are primarily overt and they have difficulties in accurately describing how they arrive at their solutions. In Piaget's system (1970), children's accounts of their covert behavior in problem solving situations are considered important because they are interpreted as providing information on the growth states of their cognitive processes and structures. In this approach, these verbalizations are also considered important because they shed light on the children's current behavior equipment (knowledge and skills) and their relevant interactional history.

The question often arises: how can a behaviorist study thinking if it is covert behavior? We can provide an answer by a detailed analysis of one form of thinking—deduction. Deduction, which is a large class of skills, can readily be made observable by asking the deducer to deduce aloud thereby making it possible to be analyzed as a behavioral sequence. We can ask questions about its components and the sequence in which they operate. We can ask questions about how deduction is learned, and better yet, how we can teach it to children who use it sparingly or poorly. We can ask what difference it makes for a person to have some representatives of this class of skills: what other behaviors become possible when this class of skill is used, relative to when it is not. As a homely and familiar example, consider the ability to extract (deduce) the square root of a number as the number that can be multiplied by itself to produce the starting number. This is the essential definition, but by no means is it a practical means of actually finding square roots. At best, it opens a process of trial-and-error, guided by our memory of the multiplication tables and the ability to extrapolate roughly from them to large numbers, and dependent on our ability to multiply accurately. Extrapolation can save some time, but nevertheless, the precise extracting of the square root of 123,456.78987654321 will still be an arduous process even by shrewd trial-and-error. A second way solves this problem. It is to teach the algorithm that yields square roots of any number of any size. We do not intend to repeat that algorithm here; only to remind you that you once knew it, perhaps still do, and at least could recover it with only a little repetition of your earlier instruction. Equipped with the algorithm—a memorized set of steps that can be applied to any number and that successively yields digit after digit of the answer—you are able to solve an infinite class of problems, the square rooting of any real number.

By teaching the first concept of square root to students, we enable them to deduce particular square roots, but poorly. In truth, we simply show them how to do trial-and-error self-multiplications strategically rather than randomly. By teaching the second method, we give our students a much quicker, as-precise-as-desired method that does not much smack of deduction. Teaching both might be said to represent good instruction: they will know how to extract an accurate square root, and also will know that it is a number that, multiplied by itself, yields the number whose square root was desired (and thus what a square root is by definition, as well as what number it is this time).

There are points to be emphasized in this lengthy example. One is that the essence of a cognitive skill, such as deduction, is an algorithm of behaviors; it is the behaviors in the correct sequence that *are* the skill. The second is that there may well be more than one algorithm underlying a given cognitive skill, and that some may be better than others. A third is that when we appreciate the algorithm, we may not always be tempted to refer to it as a *cognitive* skill, perhaps because it is so clearly understood, so obvious, so observable, and can be so external. (An unfortunate connotation of cognition is that it is internal and must be inferred rather than observed: all that is observed are the consequences in behavior of using the internal structure. When we see the behaviors themselves in their algorithm, we lose this connotation. Here, we suggest that the best connotations of cognition are its potential observability, rather than its seclusion from all but indirect inference.) A fourth point is that when we know an algorithm that constitutes a cognitive skill, we can teach the skill by teaching the algorithm. (Incidentally, the simplest algorithm for square roots is to buy an inexpensive calculator, press the buttons representing the number, and press the square-root button: the root will appear immediately, and we can simply read it off. This, too, is an algorithm, depending not on our abilities to do long division, as does the second algorithm, or shrewdly guided trial-and-error multiplication, as does the first, but rather on our ability to make the necessary amount of money, live in access to technology, translate a number into the correct sequence of button-presses, and read the answer as it appears.) So long as each algorithm is accompanied by the definition of a square root, each may be considered a cognition: no one algorithm is any more inherently cognitive than another—despite the fact that many people consider the use of the calculator as cheating. Then why not consider the use of pencil and paper with the first two as cheating as well?

Finally, there is a fifth point, not yet obvious in our example. A cognitive skill—an algorithm of behaviors—can, like any behavior, affect other behaviors in the same organism, and can affect the operation of reinforcement contingencies applied to other behaviors. Thus, we may ask you for the square root of 289, and your application of the second algorithm should, in a few minutes, yield an answer of 17. Suppose that we say, "No, that's wrong." You can check your work, response by response, in the algorithm, and check the algorithm against your memory, and finding that everything is correct, insist that 17 is correct, also. We can continue this at great length with no change in behavior by either of us; we continue to insist that you are wrong, you insist that you are correct. Thus, it may appear that your possession of the algorithm has made you immune to our instruction on this point: in effect, that we no longer can punish 17 in favor of, say, 18, which we would reinforce if you would agree to it. That is exactly what is happening—so far. But suppose a little further: if everyone else in the room says "No, it's 18;" and besides, they say, the IBM 7982 ABC Handy-Dandy computer, as used by the Computing Center to do everything from nuclear physics to our payroll, also says 18; and we express enough disgust with you for being wrong; and someone then says, sympathetically, "Oh, Sue, I know what you're doing wrong; I did the same thing three times in a row. It's the third subtrahend that throws you off," why then quite a few of us (readers and authors alike, unfortunately) will succumb (especially until we can retire in private and look up 'subtrahend'). Actual research suggests that some of us will simply give up the argument, assuming that we made an error "somewhere"; some will in fact find an error (by error, of course: the square root of 289 *is* 17); and some will, within the confines of their heads, say "It's 17 and either I'm crazy or everyone else is or this is April 1 or . . ." This third group of people nevertheless may be moved, by extreme psychological means, to finally agree that it is 18. When we disagree with the results of such procedures, we call them "brainwashing"; when we agree, we call them educational—but the point is that they exist and that they can function. In summary, then, a cognition is an algorithm of behaviors, and in principle is teachable. That algorithm may make it more or less difficult to influence its possessor by other means, just as it is difficult to coerce behavior physically when the subject is stronger than the would-be coercer. But in principle, all behavior—algorithms and aggression alike—is subject to control by environmental contingencies, and the algorithms that might insulate us from or expose us to other forms of environmental influences in principle are themselves as susceptible to control by those same kinds of influences as are more ordinary behaviors. If environmental influence keeps our algorithms strong, we may find that they help us to trace imprecise reinforcement and punishment contingencies and to react to them with better and faster behavior changes than those contingencies would produce alone. If environmental influence acts against these algorithms, then they will lose some or all of these functions.

Algorithms can be peculiarly useful behaviors, and thus peculiarly powerful behaviors, but they still are just behaviors. Nevertheless, they are one of the most neglected targets of behavior analysis that could be specified, and represent an important area for current and future research—an area that is just being broached through behavioral analyses of language.

A question to remember from this point forward is: how much of child development can we explain by using the systematic principles described here? Let us use concepts of what a child ought to be able to deduce, see, know, or understand only when we understand the experimental programs that can produce such skills and maintain their performance.

For a further discussion of a behavior analysis of problem solving and thinking, see Skinner (1969 and 1974) and Kantor and Smith (1975).

CREATIVITY

Creativity is an honorific word. It refers to interactions that are said to be beneficial to the individual, society, and even the race, and is associated with words of high esteem: intelligence, talent, ingenuity, giftedness, intuition, inventiveness, discovery, and originality.

Kantor and Smith (1975) attribute the miraculous events in civilization to creativity:

The gigantic achievements of complexly evolved civilizations with their scientific and technological competencies, local and international organizations, admired arts, and profound philosophies must in great measure be attributed to the extension of psychological behavior to cultural origins and evolutions of a social psychological type. All the miraculous happenings of human civilization must be traced back to the development by individuals of creative, imaginative, and craftsman behavior (pp. 502-503).

Skinner (1974) sees a parallel relationship between the role of creativity in changing the practices of cultures and mutations in biological evolution.

How is creativity analyzed in the framework presented here? It is one form of problem solving. It is the term applied to a class of problem solving solutions that are unusual or *original.* An original solution may be defined according to its occurrences in a group, as in normative or actuarial accounts. When a five-year-old boy arrives at a solution unusual for his age, we say he is clever; when he produces a solution unique for his age, we say he is creative. An original solution may also be defined with reference to its initial occurrence in the history of a particular person in a single problem-solving setting, or with reference to all previous problem solving settings (Goetz & Baer, 1973 and Holman, Goetz, & Baer, 1977). In research, it is not necessary that all of the problem-solving episodes under study be observed to ensure that the solution is in fact novel or original for the person.

Because we do not view a creative interaction as a mental faculty but, instead, as the behavior of an individual in relation to specific environmental circumstances, we must refer to problem-solving ability in specific terms. Thus it is meaningless to speak of a child as "creative" but meaningful to speak of a child as creative in music, painting, social affairs, science, technology, and the like.

Creative behavior can be taught. A teacher or parent can teach a child to identify and arrange conditions and response contingencies that will increase the probability of original solutions. While applied behavior research has not yet developed the details of the most expeditious procedures for teaching creative behavior in specific areas, it seems clear that such instruction should (1) help children acquire extensive abilities and knowledge repertories; (2) provide them with many opportunities, and all sorts of unusual situations, to engage in problem-solving behavior; (3) give them guidance in the techniques of approaching problems, and (4) withdraw assistance ("fade" the teaching aids) in such a way that reinforcing contingencies become a part of the problem-solving interaction itself, that is, make problem solving intrinsically reinforcing. In the process of doing so, "creative responses may be reinforced as they occur." (Goetz and Baer, 1973.)

REFERENCES

GOETZ, E.M. AND BAER, D.M., Social control of form diversity and the emergence of new forms in children's blockbuilding. *Journal of Applied Behavior Analysis,* 1973, *2,* 209-17.

HOLMAN, J., GOETZ, E.M., AND BAER, D.M., The training of creativity as an operant and an examination of its generalization characteristics. In B.C. Etzel, J.M. LeBlanc, and D.M. Baer (Eds.), *New Developments in Behavior Research: Theory, Method and Application.* Hillsdale, N.J.: Laurence Erlbaum Associates, 1977.

KANTOR, J.R. AND SMITH, N.W., *The Science of Psychology: An Interbehavioral Survey.* Chicago: Principia Press, 1975.

MILLER, N.E., Learning of visceral and glandular responses. *Science,* 1969, *163,* 434-45.

PIAGET, J., Piaget's theory. In P.H. Mussen (Ed.), *Carmichael's Manual of Child Psychology* (3rd. ed.). Vol. 1. New York: Wiley, 1970, 703-732.

SKINNER, B.F., *About Behaviorism.* New York: Knopf, 1974.

SKINNER, B.F., *Contingencies of Reinforcement: A Theoretical Analysis.* Englewood Cliffs, N.J.: Prentice-Hall, 1969.

STONE, L.J. AND CHURCH, J., *Childhood and Adolescence* (3rd. ed.). New York: Random House, 1973.

STUART, R.B. AND DAVIS, B., *Slim Chance in a Fat World: Behavioral Control of Obesity.* Champaign, Ill.: Research Press, 1972.

12

Summary

A summary of this volume can be little more than the table of contents that preceded it. It should be clear to the reader that our presentation is, in fact, only a summary of modern empirical behavior theory or behavior analysis. That is, the emphasis throughout is on empirical definitions of terms, statements of empirical principles, and explications of assumptions embodied in behaviorism. Let us, then, use the summary to emphasize the distinctive aspects of our discussion.

We have presented an outline of concepts and principles, stated in objective terms, that can be applied to behavior in general—the behavior of young and old, normal and deviant, human and animal—as it occurs in natural settings and in laboratories. A detailed application of these concepts and principles has been made to the human child, to introduce the reader to techniques of analyzing the interactions of children and their world. Such an analysis should reveal our present knowledge about the sequences of child development—knowledge that we believe to be reliable even while we have often been puzzled as to why it is true. Equally important is the point that this approach, because of its data-based orientation, should lead to the discovery of new reliable knowledge. In short, we believe that this is one way to state what we currently know about human development and to ask questions about many of the things that we do not know.

What form does this theory take? It yields a comprehensive account of the development of the human child's motor, social, perceptual, linguistic, intellectual, and motivational repertoires. Indeed, the concepts and principles that constitute the theory suggest that the foregoing developmental dimensions are arbitrary and artificial, or at least not *functional,* because they do not refer to actual events in a child's life. The discussion of the theory proceeds from simple to complex interactions in the following manner:

1. The child is conceptualized in abstract terms as a source of responses and stimuli. Responses fall into two functional categories based on *temporal* relationships: (a) respondent behaviors are controlled primarily by preceding (eliciting) stimuli and (b) operant behaviors are controlled primarily by consequent stimulation whose relationship to preceding (discriminative) stimuli is dependent on the history of behavior made in their presence. Some responses, such as the eye-blink and sphincter-control muscles, have both respondent and operant functional characteristics. Stimuli designated as organismic originate in the physical functioning and bodily activities of the child.

2. Understanding children's behavior and development requires a functional analysis of their interactions with the environment, which is conceptualized in abstract terms as the stimuli in continuous contact with the children. The environment is broken down into specific stimuli and setting events which are analyzed in terms of their functional and physical dimensions. Catalogues of the functional properties of specific stimuli, setting events, and responses are required in this analysis.

3. An analysis of development begins by describing the ways in which respondent behaviors become correlated with new (conditioned) stimuli and detached from old ones, through respondent conditioning and extinction. Descriptions are also made of the ways in which simple operant behaviors are strengthened or weakened through consequent stimuli (reinforcement), and become correlated with antecedent (discriminative) stimuli that signal occasions on which these contingencies are likely to hold. Some respondents play a major role in affective behavior and the conditioned eliciting stimuli for them may be provided by people, and hence are "social." Some of the operants are vocal, as are some of the respondents, and their discriminative, reinforcing, and conditioned eliciting properties are usually in relation to objects and the behavior of people; hence, this class of developmental interactions is "social," "cultural," and "linguistic."

4. Generalization and discrimination of stimuli and induction and differentiation of responses occur throughout all the sequences of development. Thus, children's operant and respondent behaviors

may be correlated with classes of discriminative and eliciting properties of stimuli. These classes may have varying breadth, depending on the conditioning and extinction procedures applied in natural and contrived situations. Consequently, manipulatory and verbal behaviors fall into classes called abilities and knowledge; this phenomenon, coupled with the complexity of discriminative stimuli that is possible in discriminative interactions, typically gives the label "intellectual" to such behaviors.

5. The equivalence of discriminative stimulus functions and acquired reinforcing functions suggests that many discriminative stimuli play an important role in strengthening and weakening operant behaviors in the child's future development. Some of these discriminative stimuli consist of the behavior of people (typically parents), and thus give rise to "social" reinforcers such as attention, affection, approval, achievement, pride, and status. Because social reinforcers are usually given for "social" behaviors in the presence of "social" discriminative stimuli, the development that occurs is usually described as "social" behavior or "personality."

6. In all of the above steps, scheduling of eliciting, discriminative, and reinforcing stimuli, to one another and to responses, is taken into account because they influence a child's characteristic rates of responding on a task (high versus low behavior outputs), styles of work behavior (independence versus dependence), likelihood of stopping work after reinforcement, and the durability of learned interactions (memory).

7. Most of a child's interactions in natural settings consist of complex interrelationships of respondent and operant behavior occurring in sequential units linked to each other by stimuli with reinforcing, discriminative, and eliciting functions. These units themselves have different functions in the continuous stream of interactions. The first is usually designated as having an attending function, the second a perceiving function, etc.

8. One kind of complex interaction involves conflict and decision making. These originate in situations that produce two or more stimulus consequences with opposing, contradictory, or conflictive reinforcing functions. Decision making is the process in which we assess the strengths of the opposing stimulus functions.

9. Another kind of complex interaction is emotional behavior, which is the cessation of operant behavior on the occasion of a sudden intense stimulus. Analysis takes into account the behavior preceding

the emotional event, the nature of the emotional event, the re-spondent behavior during the cessation of operant behavior, the behavior following the emotionalizing event, and the long-range effects which function as setting events.

10. Still another kind of complex interaction is self-management: in-teractions in which individuals take a hand in arranging parts of their own internal and external environments to influence their subsequent behavior in ways that have been reinforced in the past. The development of early moral behavior (conscience) and the control through feedback of physiological functioning fall into this category.

11. The concept of self-management also applies to the analysis of prob-lem solving, thinking, and creativity. In problem solving, we use self-manipulating techniques, some overt and some covert, to facilitate behaving in a way that is reinforcing to us, in this instance, reaching a solution to a confronting problem. That is, we rearrange stimuli in our internal environment, such as tracing back or recal-ling events that are relevant to the problem; and/or we rearrange stimuli in our external environment, such as transposing the problem from a symbolic to a graphical form. Thinking, like problem solving, is behavior, but is primarily covert or implicit. Problem solving refers to activities (manipulations of all sorts in-cluding thinking and reasoning) extending from simple solutions of everyday routine problems to novel solutions of problems in the arts and sciences. Arriving at novel solutions is generally called creative behavior.

Keller and Schoenfeld (1950) have written with the same objective and have stated the goal as well as we believe possible. Let us conclude, then, as they did:

The cultural environment (or, more exactly, the members of the community) starts out with a human infant formed and endowed along species lines, but capable of behavioral training in many directions. From this raw material, the culture proceeds to make, in so far as it can, a product acceptable to itself. It does this by training: by reinforcing the behavior it desires and extinguishing others; by making some natural and social stimuli into discriminative stimuli and ignoring others; by differentiating out this or that specific response or chain of responses, such as manners and attitudes; by conditioning emotional and anxiety reactions to some stimuli and not others. It teaches the individual what he may and may not do, giving him norms and ranges of social behavior that are permissive or prescriptive or prohibitive. It teaches him the language he is to speak; it gives him his standards of beauty and art, of good and bad conduct; it sets before him a picture of the ideal personality that he is to imitate and strive to be. In all this, the fundamental laws of behavior are to be found (pp. 365-66).

REFERENCES

KELLER, F.S., AND SCHOENFELD, W.N., *Principles of Psychology.* New York: Appleton-Century-Crofts, 1950.

INDEX